Contents

Introduction

Aims

The Poetry Book is part of the new EMC KS3 Series for 11 – 14 year olds. Written to address the requirements of the National Curriculum and the Framework for Teaching English, Years 7 – 9, it is a pupil book which aims to provide stimulating, surprising and thought-provoking texts and activities on poetry. Activities are structured to fit approximately one hour lessons and most of the units are designed to last three to four weeks. The units aim to foreground the following elements of effective teaching:

- a fast pace and strong focus
- varied teaching styles and pupil groupings
- active approaches to texts
- shared reading and writing
- opportunities for guided reading and writing.

Balancing range and progression

The book offers a choice of up to four units for each year. Each year includes a stimulating variety of poetry, both pre-twentieth century and contemporary, from the English Literary Heritage and other cultures. 'I saw a child' focuses on a collection of poems on a theme while 'A Poetry Reading Trail' explores the way a single story has been re-told in poetry through the ages. Three of the units focus on the work of one poet: John Agard, John Hegley and Sophie Hannah. The 'John Hegley' and 'Sophie Hannah' units include readings and interviews on the video, while John Agard performs his poems, without interview material. 'Poems on the Box' and 'Lit Pops' look at the different ways poetry has been presented in sound and images. The most challenging unit 'Sonnets' focuses on a single poetic form and looks towards the types of reading and writing pupils will be expected to tackle for GCSE English Literature. 'Words and Images' includes 9 full colour paintings as a stimulus for pupils own creative writing and provides an alternative way into the critical exploration of Blake's poem 'A Poison Tree'.

The video includes readings and discussion by the three poets, short sequences of moving images for creative writing activities and a selection of programmes from the BBC series *Poems on the Box* and the Channel 4 series, *Lit Pops*.

As a whole, the poems and activities cover a wide range of teaching objectives, building progression into the skills of speaking, listening, reading and writing over a three year course. The order of the units in the pupil book reflects this sense of progression. Although units have been devised to address the different objectives of Years 7, 8 and 9, no mention is made of the Framework in the pupil book and units are not allocated to a particular year. This information is provided in the Teachers' notes on the CD Rom. This is to enable teachers to adapt the material for a different year group, or make changes to fulfil different or additional objectives.

Teachers' notes

To support the teaching of these units, teachers' notes consist of:

- long, medium and short term plans for each unit, written to the Framework
- additional language notes
- pupil charts
- copies of some key texts to allow for photocopying and annotation. These can also be made into OHTs for whole class work.

For maximum flexibility these are published on a CD Rom so that they can be printed off or amended as required. Updates in response to changes in national policy will be published on the English and Media Centre's free website (www.englishandmedia.co.uk).

Additional support for teaching terminology can be found on the 'Standards' pages of the DfEE website (www.standards.dfee.gov.uk/literacy/glossary).

4

THE POETRY BOOK

ENGLISH & MEDIA CENTRE

EMC KS3 ENGLISH SERIES

Acknowledgements

Written and edited by Barbara Bleiman, with Lucy Webster
Additional material by Sabrina Broadbent
Additional editorial support: Guido Martini and Kate Domaille
Design: Eamonn England
Additional design: Fran Stowell
Video: Michael Simons
Video Graphics: Yan Masterman
Book and video cover: Blaise Thompson
Printed by Giunti Industrie Grafiche, Prato-Italy
Published by: English & Media Centre © 2001
ISBN: 0 907016 73 1

Thanks to John Agard, Sophie Hannah and John Hegley for their generous support of this project and to Penny Downes and the pupils of Morpeth School, Tower Hamlets; Paul Wright and the pupils of Acland Burghley School, Camden; Iain Bruce and the pupils of The Latymer School, Enfield; Dave Sheppard and the pupils of The Charter School, Southwark and Jane Bassett and the pupils of Stoke Newington School, Hackney for help in piloting the material.

Thanks also to: John Agard and the Caroline Sheldon Agency for poems from Wanted Man, Limbo Dancer in Dark Glasses (Serpent's Tail), We Animals Would Like a Word With You (Red Fox), You'll Love This Stuff (Cambridge University Press) and Get Back Pimple (Puffin); the BBC for Poems on the Box; Channel 4 for Lit Pops; PFD on behalf of Adrian Mitchell for 'Icarus Shmicarus' from Heart on the Left (Bloodaxe), Roger McGough for '40-love' from After the Merrymaking (Penguin) © Roger McGough and James Fenton for 'I saw a child' from Out of Danger (Penguin); Bloodaxe Books and Fleur Adcock for an extract from 'Toads' from The Incident Book; Carcanet and Sophie Hannah for poems from The Hero and the Girl, Next Door, Leaving and Leaving You and Hotels Like Houses, Edwin Morgan for 'Glasgow Sonnet' and 'Glasgow 5 March' from Collected Poems; Eavan Boland for 'This Moment' from Collected Poems and James Tate for 'Five Years Old' from Collected Poems; Faber and Faber and Simon Armitage for 'Poem' from Kid, Ted Hughes for 'Full Moon and Little Frieda' from Wodwo, Don Paterson for 'The Work' from The Eyes and W.H. Auden for 'Who's Who' from The Collected Poems; Dorothy Hewett and the Poetry Society for 'Exodus', first published from The Poetry Review, Spring 1999; HarperCollins and Gareth Owen for 'Icarus by Mobile'; Longman Books and Isobel Thrilling for 'Children in Wartime'; Independiente and Travis for the video of 'Driftwood', lyrics to 'Driftwood' by Fran Healy reproduced by kind permission Sony/ATV Music Publishing; John Hegley and Methuen Publishing Ltd for poems from Beyond Our Kennel (1998), The Family Pack (1996); Glad to Wear Glasses (1990); Random House and Frances Cornford for 'Childhood' from Collected Poems; Patience Agbabi for 'Ufo Woman'; Patience Agbabi and Canongate Books for 'North(west)ern'; U.A. Fanthorpe for 'Needle Work' and 'The Sheepdog' from Voices Off (1984) reproduced by permission of Peterloo Poets; Elizabeth Barnett for 'Sonnet xlii' from The Collected Sonnets by Edna St. Vincent Millay; Carol Ann Duffy for 'Mrs Icarus' from The World's Wife and Billy Collins for 'On Turning Ten' from Taking Off Emily Dickinson's Clothes, reproduced by permission of Picador Books; Brian Patten for 'Gust Becos I Cud Not Spel' from Gargling With Jelly, Jackie Kay for 'The Adventures of Carla Johnson' from Two's Company and James Berry for 'Bits of Early Days' from Playing a Dazzler, reproduced by permission of Penguin Books; Musees Royaux des Beaux-Arts de Belgique, Brussels/Bridgeman Art Library for Landscape with the Fall of Icarus by Pieter the Elder Brueghel and Bridgeman Art Library and artist for The Fall of Icarus by Andre Durand; Weeping Woman by Pablo Picasso, © Succession Picasso/DACS 2001; On the Balcony by Peter Blake, © Peter Blake 2001; The Snack Bar by Edward Burra, © care of Alex Read and Levfevre, London; The Painter's Family by Georgio de Chirico, © DACS 2001; Landscape From a Dream by Paul Nash, Fishermen at Sea by J.M.W. Turner and The Body of Abel Found by Adam and Eve by William Blake © Tate, 2001; A Jan Steen Kitchen by Leaman, courtesy the Beaux Arts Gallery, London; Rain by Howard Hodgkin, © the artist; the Wallace Collection, London for A Lady Reading a Letter, Gerard ter Borch; Ashmolean Museum Oxford for Home from the Sea, Arthur Hughes; Blaise Thompson for 4 original paintings on 'A Poison Tree' in Unit 5.

What is a poem?

Talking about poems

Poems on the page   Group work

Here is the beginning of a poem that you may have come across before. It is written without any punctuation.

> 'Twas brillig and the slithy toves did gyre and gimble in the wabe all mimsy were the borogoves and the mome raths outgrabe beware the Jabberwock my son the jaws that bite the claws that catch beware the Jubjub bird and shun the frumious Bandersnatch he took his vorpal sword in hand long time the manxome foe he sought so rested he by the Tumtum tree and stood awhile in thought

- Try turning it back into the layout of poetry, deciding where to start a new line and how to punctuate it.

- Talk about what helped you make your decisions.

Here is another poem, written as prose.

> ## Toads
>
> Let's be clear about this I love toads so when I found our old one dying washed into the drain by flood-water in the night and then if I can bring myself to say it scalded by soapy lather I myself had let out of the sink we suffered it through together it was the summer of my father's death I saw his spirit in every visiting creature in every small thing at risk of harm bird moth butterfly beetle the black rabbit lolloping along concrete lost in suburbia and our toad

You may find it harder to decide on line breaks for this one!

- Spend 5 –10 minutes having a go at it.

- When you've spent a bit of time trying to decide, talk about what the problems were.

■   Now look at the extracts from the poems as they were written by the poets on page 11.

■   Talk about what you have learned from doing this activity about the shape and form of poems.

What is a poem?   Pair and class work
Printed below and over the page are extracts from different kinds of texts. Some are poems, some are not. They have all been printed in the same form, without the original line breaks and without punctuation.

■   In pairs, read through them. Decide which ones you think you would describe as poetry.

■   Take it in turns to offer suggestions and reasons for your views, as a whole class.

1. 40 love middle aged couple playing tennis when the game ends and they go home the net will still be between them

2. one day the phone rang and a little boy answered may I speak to your parents they're busy oh is anybody else there the police can I speak to them they're busy oh is anybody else there the firemen can I speak to them they're busy so let me get this straight your parents, the police, and the firemen are there but they're all busy what are they doing looking for me

3. once driven forever smitten

4. Humpty Dumpty sat on the wall Humpty Dumpty had a great fall all the King's horses all the King's men couldn't put Humpty together again.

5. eat football sleep football drink Coca Cola

6. so let freedom ring from the prodigious hilltops of New Hampshire let freedom ring from the mighty mountains of New York let freedom ring from the heightening Alleghenies of Pennsylvania let freedom ring from the snowcapped Rockies of Colorado let freedom ring from the curvacious peaks of California but not only that let freedom ring from Stone Mountain of Georgia let freedom ring from lookout Mountain of Tennessee let freedom ring from every hill and molehill of Mississippi from every mountainside let freedom ring

7. I cannot see what flowers are at my feet nor what soft incense hangs upon the boughs but in embalmèd darkness guess each sweet wherewith the seasonable month endows the grass the thicket and the fruit-tree wild white hawthorn and the pastoral eglantine fast-fading violets covered up in leaves and mid-May's eldest child the coming musk-rose full of dewy wine the murmurous haunt of flies on summer eves

8. a soft fall rain slips down through the trees and the smell of the ocean is so strong that it can almost be licked off the air trucks rumble along Rogers Street and men in t-shirts stained with fishblood shout to each other from the decks of boats beneath them the ocean swells up against the black pilings and sucks back down to the barnacles beer cans and old pieces of styrofoam rise and fall and pools of spilled diesel fuel undulate like huge iridescent jellyfish the boats rock and creak against their ropes and seagulls complain and hunker down and complain some more

9. an hour is a sea between a few and me with them would harbour be

- Now look at them as they were originally published on pages 12-13. Does this make you change your mind about any of them? If so, which ones and why?

Your teacher will tell you which of the extracts are taken from poems.

- Talk about anything that strikes you as interesting or surprising. Do any of the extracts which are not from poems share any of the features of poems? (For example do any of them use rhyme or have a regular rhythm? Do any of them use language in 'poetic' ways?)

- Sum up your ideas on:
  - what you think makes poetry special
  - what other kinds of writing have similar kinds of features to poetry.

What poets say   Group work

The quotation bubbles on pages 8 and 9 show what some poets and readers think poetry is.

- Read each one in turn and talk about the different ideas suggested.

- Then choose the three comments which you like most. Talk about why you think they are interesting or important. Find one quotation from the poem extracts you looked at, to support each comment.

1. Poetry's like a huge multi coloured marquee that has room for all kinds of forms and voices. (Vicki Feaver)

2. Every poem is an island. To get to a poem requires sailing out from the mainland of routine language. Some poems are close to shore, others much further away … A poem is defined by the rugged shore of its right hand margin, cutting it off from prose. (Robert Crawford)

3. A poem should not mean but be. (Archibald Macleish)

4. I started writing poetry because I didn't like poetry. (Benjamin Zephaniah)

5. Poetry is a hotline to the emotions. (Andrew Motion)

6. Poetry, like music, is to be heard. (Basil Bunting)

7. Poetry is language in orbit. (Seamus Heaney)

8. The best craftsmanship always leaves holes and gaps in the works of the poem so that something that is not in the poem can creep, crawl, flash or thunder in. (Dylan Thomas)

9. Prose = words in their best order; poetry = the best words in their best order. (Samuel Taylor Coleridge)

10. Poetry is 'language on a spree'. (John Hegley)

11. Poetry is language made strange. (Cox Report)

12. Rap music is deeply poetic. (William Sieghart)

Summing up your ideas   Individual work

■   Use all the ideas you have been exploring to write a paragraph on what *you* think poetry is or isn't. Make use of any words and phrases written by other people, to help you. Use your writing as a way of sorting out your ideas.

Here's how one KS3 pupil started her paragraph:

Poetry doesn't have to rhyme but it does have to sound good. It uses language in special ways. For instance...

Choosing a poem

■ In pairs, spend some time browsing through a selection of poetry books and poetry websites.

■ Make a note of any poems which you particularly like or which you find striking for some reason.

■ Choose one of the poems and write a short explanation of why you chose it.
You could think about:
  – its subject
  – any patterns you notice (For example, does it rhyme? Does it have a regular rhythm? Is it divided into verses? If it is, does each verse explore a different part of the subject?)
  – how it sounds when you read it out loud (for example, it might sound like a speaking voice or like a song)
  – the images
  – whether it is funny or serious, sad or silly
  – what it means to you.

Presenting your poems   Class work
■ Take it in turns to introduce your poems to the class. You could record the poems on video to introduce other pupils to poetry.

Making an anthology   Individual work
■ Write out your chosen poem and an explanation of why you chose it.

■ Collect all the poems together into a class anthology, so that you can read each others' choices.

Texts as published

Jabberwocky

'Twas brillig, and the slithy toves
    Did gyre and gimble in the wabe;
All mimsy were the borogoves,
      And the mome raths outgrabe.

'Beware the Jabberwock, my son!
    The jaws that bite, the claws that catch!
Beware the Jubjub bird, and shun
      The frumious Bandersnatch!'

He took his vorpal sword in hand:
    Long time the manxome foe he sought-
So rested he by the Tumtum tree,
      And stood awhile in thought.

Toads

Let's be clear about this: I love toads.

So when I found our old one dying,
 washed into the drain by flood-water
in the night and then – if I can bring myself
to say it – scalded by soapy lather
I myself had let out of the sink,
we suffered it through together.

It was the summer of my father's death.
I saw his spirit in every visiting creature,
in every small thing at risk of harm:
bird, moth, butterfly, beetle,
the black rabbit lolloping along concrete,
lost in suburbia; and our toad.

Fleur Adcock

1.

40-love

middle	aged
couple	playing
ten-	nis
when	the
game	ends
and	they
go	home
the	net
will	still
be	bet-
tween	them

2.

One day, the phone rang, and a little boy answered.
"May I speak to your parents?"
"They're busy."
"Oh. Is anybody else there?"
"The police."
"Can I speak to them?"
"They're busy."
"Oh. Is anybody else there?"
"The firemen."
"Can I speak to them?"
"They're busy."
"So let me get this straight – your parents, the police,
and the firemen are there, but they're all busy? What are they doing?"
"Looking for me."

3.

Once driven, forever smitten

4.

Humpty Dumpty sat on the wall
Humpty Dumpty had a great fall
All the King's horses
All the King's men
Couldn't put Humpty together again.

5.

Eat football. Sleep football. Drink Coca Cola

6.

So let freedom ring from the prodigious hilltops of New Hampshire. Let freedom ring from the mighty mountains of New York. Let freedom ring from the heightening Alleghenies of Pennsylvania!

Let freedom ring from the snowcapped Rockies of Colorado!

Let freedom ring from the curvacious peaks of California!

But not only that; let freedom ring from Stone Mountain of Georgia!

Let freedom ring from Lookout Mountain of Tennessee!

Let freedom ring from every hill and molehill of Mississippi. From every mountainside, let freedom ring.

7.

I cannot see what flowers are at my feet,
    Nor what soft incense hangs upon the boughs,
But, in embalmèd darkness, guess each sweet
    Wherewith the seasonable month endows
The grass, the thicket, and the fruit-tree wild –
  White hawthorn, and the pastoral eglantine;
   Fast-fading violets covered up in leaves;
   And mid-May's eldest child,
The coming musk-rose, full of dewy wine,
   The murmurous haunt of flies on summer eves.

8.

A soft fall rain slips down through the trees and the smell of the ocean is so strong that it can almost be licked off the air. Trucks rumble along Rogers Street and men in t-shirts stained with fishblood shout to each other from the decks of boats. Beneath them the ocean swells up against the black pilings and sucks back down to the barnacles. Beer cans and old pieces of styrofoam rise and fall and pools of spilled diesel fuel undulate like huge iridescent jellyfish. The boats rock and creak against their ropes and seagulls complain and hunker down and complain some more.

9.

An Hour is a Sea
Between a few and me –
With them would Harbor be –

Words and images

In this unit you will:
- use visual images as a stimulus for your own poetry writing
- use visual images to help you read and analyse a poem
- look at ways in which poems have been presented visually on TV
- create your own presentation of a poem using sound and images.

Poems and paintings

Drafting a poem Group and Individual work

■ Look at the paintings on pages 15 – 20. Pick the 3 or 4 paintings you are most interested in. For each of these think of:
- a title for the painting
- one image to describe something about the painting
- three adjectives to describe the mood.

■ In groups of 3 or 4 talk a bit about the paintings you picked. Describe what you think is going on in the painting. Compare the adjectives you chose to describe its mood.

■ Now choose one of the paintings as the stimulus for writing a poem.

■ Choose one of these ways of using the painting to help you draft a poem.

Collect together a list of images to describe what you see. You could borrow the ones that other people in the class have created, as well as finding ones of your own. Choose the best ones and decide on a sequence for them, as a first draft of a poem.	Pick one of the people in the painting and write a monologue in his or her voice, describing things from his or her point of view.	Tell the story of the painting, in poetry. Start by thinking about what's happening in it and what might have happened before or after that moment.
Choose a form, such as a sonnet, a haiku or a poem in quatrains (4 line stanzas). Describe the painting but make it fit the form.	Imagine yourself in the painting. Where would you be? What would you be feeling? Write a poem with each line starting with 'I' or 'My'. Write it in the present tense and try to convey feelings and emotions.	Look back at the titles you gave to the paintings. Choose one of the titles and use it as a starting point for a poem, not necessarily about that particular painting.

■ Follow this pattern to write your poem.

- First brainstorm some ideas.
- Then write a first draft.
- Show it to someone else in your class and ask them to annotate it, with things that work especially well and things that you might change.
- Show it to a second reader. Ask them to comment on what you've written and on the comments of the first reader.
- Write a final version of your poem, to be displayed on your classroom wall. If you can, design it on a computer, choosing a font that will bring out the qualities of what you have written.

Rain, 1984-9 (Oil on wood, support 1640mm x 1795mm x 51mm) by Howard Hodgkin (1932-). © the artist

Weeping Woman, 1937 (Pencil and crayon on paper. support 292mm x 232mm) by Pablo Picasso (1881-1973). © Succession Picasso/DACS 2001

A Lady Reading a Letter, Early 1660s (Canvas. relined;(H) 44.2cm. (W) 32.2cm) by Gerard ter Borch reproduced by permission of the Wallace Collection. London

Writing poems

Fishermen at Sea, exhibited 1796. (Oil on canvas: support 914mm x 1222mm) by J.M.W. Turner (1775-1851). © Tate. 2001

Landscape From a Dream, 1936-8 (Oil on canvas: support 679mm x 1016mm) by Paul Nash (1889-1946). © Tate. 2001

Writing poems

The Snack Bar, 1930, (Oil on canvas; support 762mm x 559mm) by Edward Burra, © care of Alex Read and Lefevre, London

Writing poems

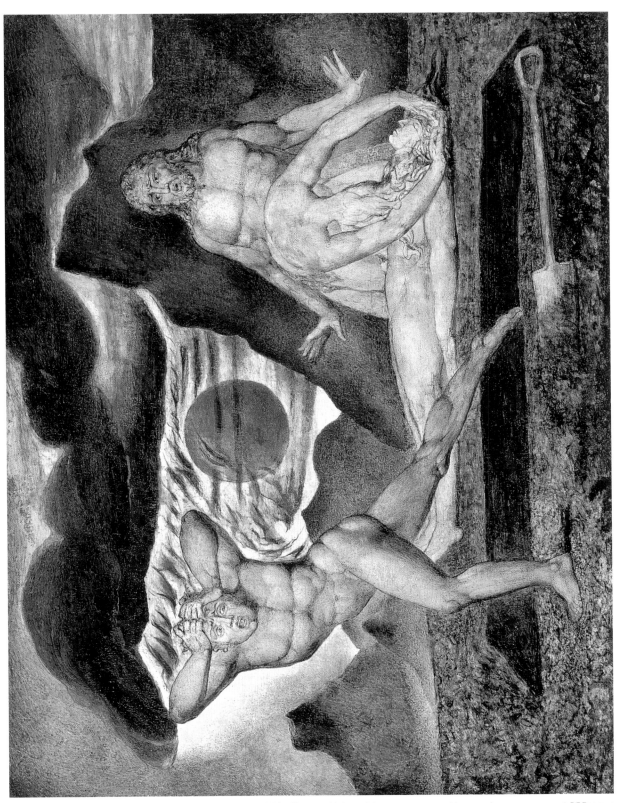

The Body of Abel Found by Adam and Eve, circa 1826. (Pen and ink and tempera over gold on mahogany; support 325mm x 433mm) by William Blake (1757-1827). © Tate. 2001

Home From Sea by Arthur Hughes, reproduced by permission of the Ashmolean Museum, University of Oxford

A Jan Steen Kitchen, 1995-6 (Oil on canvas, support 1235mm x 1705mm), by Jonathon Leaman (1954-), courtesy of the Beaux Arts Gallery, London

Writing poems

William Blake's 'A Poison Tree'

Exploring the title   Class work
■   Talk about the associations conjured up for you by the title 'A Poison Tree'. What expectations do you have of a poem with this title?

Looking at images
The artist Blaise Thompson was asked to paint a series of images in response to Blake's poem 'A Poison Tree'. They are printed on pages 22 and 23.

■   Study the paintings carefully and, with a partner, talk about each one. You could think about: what the picture is of; the mood; the colours.

■   Add any more ideas you now have about the poem they are a response to.

Reading the poem
■   Now read the poem, printed below.

> # A Poison Tree
>
> I was angry with my friend:
> I told my wrath, my wrath did end.
> I was angry with my foe:
> I told it not, my wrath did grow.
>
> And I water'd it in fears,
> Night and morning with my tears;
> And I sunned it with smiles,
> And with soft deceitful wiles.
>
> And it grew both day and night,
> Till it bore an apple bright;
> And my foe beheld it shine,
> And he knew that it was mine.
>
> And into my garden stole
> When the night had veil'd the pole:
> In the morning glad I see
> My foe outstretch'd beneath the tree.
>
> **William Blake**

■   Tell each other the story of what is going on in this poem.

Poets often use a story to explore difficult themes, emotions and relationships.

■   What do you think Blake is writing about in 'A Poison Tree'?

■   In what ways are these themes reflected in the paintings?

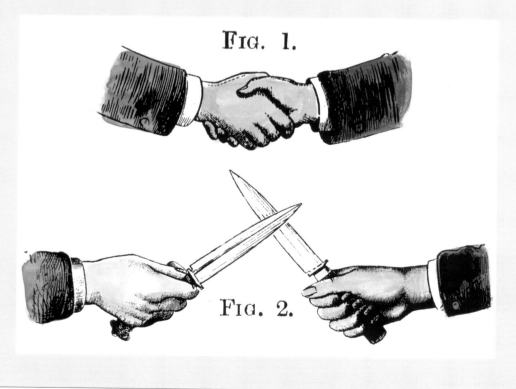

Fig. 1.

Fig. 2.

Original paintings on 'A Poison Tree' by Blaise Thompson, © the artist, 2001

William Blake was not only a poet. He was also an engraver. All the poems in the collection *Songs of Innocence and Experience* from which 'A Poison Tree' is taken, are accompanied by an engraving. The one for 'A Poison Tree' is reproduced below.

- Talk about the relationship between the poem and the engraving. What insights, if any, does the engraving give you into the poem?

Representing an emotion Individual work and Homework

- Draw or sketch or paint something to represent an emotion, for example, love, jealousy, guilt or fear.

- Use your drawing as the starting point for writing a poem exploring this emotion. Try and write the poem using the same style and form as Blake's 'A Poison Tree'.

Poems on the Box

In 1993 the BBC broadcast a series of short programmes called *Poems on the Box*. Each programme took one poem and presented it using a combination of sound and pictures. Some of the poems were read by the poet or an actor, others were presented with sound effects or as words on the screen only. The titles of the poems are listed here in the order they appear on the video.

40-Love	Roger McGough
Dis Poetry	Benjamin Zephaniah
Sea Fever	John Masefield
Magnetic	Wendy Cope
Bus Drivers' Prayer	Traditional
This is Just to Say	William Carlos Williams

Watching *Poems on the Box* Class viewing

- Watch the poems for a first time without making notes.

- Talk about which 'Poem on the box' you enjoyed most on this first viewing.

- Watch the poems again, this time making a note of the different techniques used to represent the poem. Use the headings listed here to help you organise your notes.

  - Font (size, style)
  - The way the words of the poem are shown on the screen
  - Colour
  - Images
  - Music
  - Other sound effects
  - Voice over

You might choose to focus on the two or three poems which had most impact on you when you saw them for the first time.

- Talk about how well the representation captures what is special about the poem (for example, its sound, meaning and tone).

Writing about one 'Poem on the Box'   Individual work

- Focus on one of the poems. Write a short piece explaining how it is represented on *Poems on the Box* and why this presentation is effective. Suggest any ideas you have for other ways this could be done.

Your poem on the box   Group work

- Choose a poem which you think would make a good 'poem on the box'. You could spend some time browsing through poetry books.

- On sheets of A4 or A3 paper, sketch out your ideas for how the poem could be represented visually. Annotate it to show the effects you want to create. For example, you might want to use a flashing, coloured font in a poem about fireworks.

- Use the EMC *Picture Power* programme or Microsoft *Powerpoint* to create a rough draft of your own poem on the box.

- Write a commentary explaining what you were trying to do.

Using images for creative writing

This section gives you the chance to focus on a short piece of film as a stimulus for writing a poem of your own. The titles are: Zoo, Chinese New Year, Waterfall and Escalator.

Watching the film   Class viewing

- Work through the sequence suggested here to help you shape your ideas into a poem.

  - Watch the video for a first time without writing.

  - Make a note of your first thoughts, ideas and impressions. Record your ideas as single words or phrases. Concentrate particularly on adjectives to describe what you see and verbs to describe actions.

  - Watch the video again. This time concentrate on words focusing on the five senses: sight, touch, taste, sound, smell.

  - Watch the video one last time. This time concentrate on finding a point of view from which to write the poem. You could also think about the voice you will write in. Will it be your own? Or will you tell it from the point of view and in the voice of someone or something in the film? This could even be the person behind the camera!

  - Look at your collection of words and phrases. Try and come up with additions and alternatives for these words. Use a thesaurus to help you.

  - Begin to note down ideas for how you could use these words and ideas in your poem. For example, would a descriptive or narrative poem be more appropriate?

  - Write a first draft of the poem. Remember the video you have watched is only the starting point for your writing. You might choose to write about something completely different, using the words you have collected as a metaphor for something else.

26

John Agard

In this unit you will:
- use an active reading approach to help you explore and get to grips with a poem
- recognise what makes the style and approach of John Agard's poetry special
- learn how to explain how a writer has achieved particular effects
- express a personal viewpoint on poetry
- write your own poems, based on your reading of Agard's poems.

John Agard on video

Before watching the video Group work

In the boxes below are a few lines and phrases from poems by the poet John Agard.

■   Read the fragments and talk about what you expect his poems to be like. Jot down a few notes, using the prompts below. You'll come back to your notes later.

- What kinds of subjects will they deal with?
- What kind of style will they be written in?
- What can you tell about the poet?
- Do you think they will be lively, funny, formal, simple, traditional, playful, serious, intense, light-hearted, thought-provoking, angry, chatty or direct?

1.
When you see
de rainbow
you know

2.
I only armed wit mih human breath
but human breath
is a dangerous weapon

3.
Tell me if Ah seeing right
Take a look down de street

4.
Oh my beautiful fat wife

5.
Words dancin
words dancin
till dey sweat
words like fishes
jumpin out a net

6.
But listen Mr Oxford don

The voice of the poem

A poetry performance Class viewing

■ Watch John Agard read his poems on the video.

■ Spend a couple of minutes talking about your response to the poems and the performance. What did you most enjoy? What did you find most memorable? Jot down four or five adjectives to describe John Agard's performance. How do these words match up with the words you chose to describe your expectations of the poems?

Choosing a favourite poem   Individual work

■ Choose the poem that you liked best. Think briefly about what you liked about it, jotting down a few ideas on a piece of paper. The spidergram below shows one way of doing it. You could look at the text of the poem on pages 37– 41 to help you.

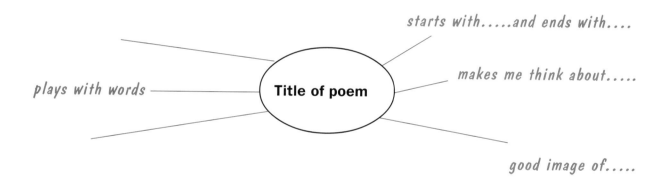

starts with.....and ends with....

makes me think about.....

Title of poem

plays with words

good image of.....

Just a minute   Pair work

■ Try talking to your partner about your poem, for one whole minute, without stopping.

Poems and performance 'Poetry Jump-up'   Group viewing and class work

John Agard is a powerful performer of his own poetry. He is well known for writing poems that work well when read aloud.

■ Watch 'Poetry Jump-up' again on the video. Each group should take responsibility for thinking about one of these aspects of the poem as a performance.

  – How important is the rhythm? How does his performance emphasise it?
  – How important is rhyme? What do you notice about the ways he uses it?

28

- How much repetition does he use (of words and whole phrases or lines)?
- In what ways does he use sounds to make a strong impact? You should think about his use of techniques such as: alliteration (when the same consonant sound is repeated, usually at the beginning of words); assonance (when the same vowel sounds are repeated in words that are close together); onomatopoeia (words which imitate the sound they are describing, like 'crash', 'slither' and 'zip').
- How do his voice, facial gestures and body language contribute to the performance?
- How do the graphics and use of images on the video contribute to the performance?

■ Spend a few minutes in your groups collecting together your observations ready to report back to the class.

■ Share the small groups' observations as a whole class.

■ Sum up the ways in which John Agard's poetry suits being performed to an audience.

Performing another poem   Pair or group work
'Five Deities' and 'Not-Enough-Pocket-Money Blues' on pages 40 and 41 are two poems by John Agard that do not appear on the video.

■ Now that you have talked about the way 'Poetry Jump-up' works as a performance, choose one of these poems to prepare for performance.

■ In pairs or small groups, talk about the poem and how you might go about performing it to bring it to life. You should think about how John Agard has used rhythm, language, repetitions and sounds to create the meaning and mood of the poem. How will you use your own style and voice(s)?

■ Spend some time practising your performance. Experiment with:
  - movements and gestures
  - loud and quiet voices
  - changing the speaker at key moments
  - having more than one voice at different times
  - finding ways of emphasising the rhythm.

■ Do your performances in front of the whole class.

Digging deeper

Work through this sequence of activities to allow you to think in more detail about how John Agard has crafted his poems and what makes them special.

Playing with words Group work
- Collect 2 or 3 examples from Agard's poems that show how the poet uses different kinds of word play, for example:
  - inventing words
  - playing with sounds
  - using puns (words with more than one meaning)
  - using rhyme in humorous ways.

What's it all about?   Individual and class work
- Choose one poem. Try to answer the questions listed here.

  - What's it all about?
  - Why do you think John Agard wrote it?
  - What does it leave you thinking about or thinking *differently* about?

- Feed back your views on the ideas in the poems.

John Agard's voice   Group and class work

One of the features of John Agard's poetry that you might have noticed is his voice. Agard, who was born in Guyana, is part of a rich modern tradition of British poets, originally from the Caribbean, who have celebrated their language through poetry. Agard gives his poems the quality of his own speech. He tries to capture his spoken voice in writing.

- To think about how he does this, watch 'Rainbow' on the video again. Now look at it on the page. Brainstorm everything you notice about the ways the writing conveys his spoken voice. For instance, what's special about the way he uses grammar (verbs, tenses and pronouns in particular)?

Thinking about language
The quotations on the next page are taken from reviews of John Agard's poetry. They suggest what each reviewer found distinctive about the way Agard writes.

- Find short extracts from the poems which seem to you to illustrate what is being said in these comments. Use them to help you come up with your own descriptions of his poetry.

steeped in the rhythms of the West Indies

the wonderful Creole poet, performer and storyteller

as direct as the voice in the bus queue

a poetry boundary pusher

his attempts to express such a wide range of subject matter using Creole is an important contribution to Caribbean poetic forms

rhythmic, flavourful, colourful and vibrant

a special mixture of African and European styles

his poetry reflects something of the rhythms of his Caribbean background

the music of the soul

his poetry fills a deep need within us all for rhythm and language

poetry can change the world we see into something new

inventive poems

some of the poems … sing and you can read them as though you were listening to a catchy song. Others speak to you and urge you to think, to meditate on an atmosphere or feeling

English or Englishes?

Standard English, dialect and accent are all words connected with the way we use the English language in speech and in writing. Printed below are some definitions of Standard English, accent and dialect. There is also another term which you might find helpful when thinking about how to describe John Agard's poetry: creole.

■   Read the different definitions.

Dialect

The term dialect refers to any variety of a language used by a group of speakers. It refers to the content of the utterance rather than the pronunciation.

There are two main types of dialect in English:
- Regional varieties which relate to a geographical area.
- Standard English which is used by speakers and writers in any area.

A language variety in which the use of grammar and vocabulary identify the regional or social background of the speaker.

Accent

Features of pronunciation which vary according to the speaker's regional and social origin. All oral language including standard English is spoken with an accent. The term accent refers to pronunciation only.

Standard English

Standard English is the variety of English used in public communication, particularly in writing. It is the form taught in schools. It is not limited to a particular region and can be spoken with any accent. There are differences in vocabulary and grammar between standard English and other varieties. Note that standard British English is not the only standard variety; other English speaking countries, such as the United States and Australia have their own standard varieties.

The term 'Standard English' refers to a dialect which has acquired the status of representing the English language.

Creole

A mother tongue formed from the contact of a European language with another one, especially an African one.

■   Talk about these definitions and make sure you're clear about each of the terms.

■   Identify some of the ways John Agard has tried to capture his accent (i.e. the way he pronounces words) in his written language.

■   Make a list of some of the ways in which the language in John Agard's poetry is different from written standard English.

■   Choose a short extract from 'Rainbow' or one of the other poems you have particularly enjoyed listening to. Try and re-write the lines in formal Standard English. The following example shows you the sort of thing you could do.

I does want know
if God
ain't a woman

I would like to know
whether God is a woman

- What difference does it make to write the poetry in standard English? What is lost from the poem? You could think about the way it sounds (the rhythm, the words which get emphasised and so on), the meaning and the impact on the reader.

- What is the effect of using dialect in this poem? Why do you think the poet chose to use it?

- Take it in turns to report your discussions on Agard's language and use of dialect.

What's special about John Agard's poetry?   Individual and class work
- Look back at the notes you took before you watched the video, when you shared expectations of the poems. Talk about whether your expectations have been confirmed or challenged. Is there anything you would like to add now?

- Decide what you think are the three most important features of Agard's poems. Write three comments about them, using this structure:

  I think John Agard's poetry is............because......... An example of this is............

- Take it in turns to read out your statements.

Writing in your voice   Individual and group work
- Choose one short section from any of Agard's poems. Try writing it in your own spoken voice. See whether you can capture the sound of your voice – your accent, any features of your own dialect or teenage spoken language. Use the following to help you:
  - layout
  - punctuation
  - non-standard spellings
  - words or phrases that are normally only spoken, not written (such as 'y'know').

- Read your version to a small group, then show them how you have written it down. Offer each other suggestions for ways of capturing your spoken language in writing more clearly.

- For homework write a final version of your poem.

A close focus on 'Listen Mr. Oxford don'

'Listen Mr. Oxford don' is perhaps the most challenging and complex poem in this selection. You might find it helpful to look back at the definitions of standard English, accent and dialect on page 32 before you watch John Agard read the poem again.

- Look at the photographs below of Oxford taken at a University graduation ceremony. Suggest adjectives to describe the place and the people.

Watching the video   Class viewing

- Now watch John Agard performing the poem on the video.

What point is Agard making?
- Talk about these words and phrases and what associations they have for you:

  Oxford don
  The Queen's English
  accessory to my offence
  syntax
  grammar
  Oxford dictionary
  inciting [...] to riot
  present tense
  serve time
  mugging
  assault

- Can you split these words into two separate groups, each from a different area of life? What are they? What does putting these two groups of words together suggest about the subject of the poem?

- Look at how John Agard puts different kinds of language together. Talk about each of the phrases on the next page, using the questions to help you think about the point Agard is trying to make.

What is the Queen's English? How does it compare with the narrator's English?

mugging de Queen's English
is the story of my life

Dem accuse me of assault
on de Oxford dictionary/

Who's 'dem'?

What does the Oxford dictionary stand for?

I only armed wit mih human breath
but human breath
is a dangerous weapon

How might breath be a weapon?

I slashing suffix in self-defence
I bashing future wit present tense

Why 'future' and 'suffix'? (A suffix is what's added to the end of words e.g. -ed, -ful, -ness)

Satire

Satire is where someone or something is made fun of, as a way of criticising it. Satire is usually used to criticise something important or powerful. It often works by:
- exaggeration
- putting together two things that normally don't go together, in surprising or shocking ways (incongruity)
- saying one thing when you mean the opposite (irony)
- taking very seriously something that is obviously ridiculous.

■ Do you think 'Listen Mr. Oxford don' is a satire? Is it criticising something powerful? Look for examples of the techniques listed above to help you decide.

Writing about 'Listen Mr Oxford don'   Homework

■ Write a few paragraphs about the poem. You should include some comments on the following:
- what the poem is about
- what point you think it is making (that is, what do you think Agard wants the reader to think about?)
- how Agard uses language to emphasise the point he is making
- what you found interesting about it and why (or why not).

■ Give short examples and quotations from the poem to try to explain your views.

Writing your own poems

■ Choose one of the poetry writing suggestions in the box below and work through the stages suggested here.

- First brainstorm some ideas.
- Then write a first draft.
- Show it to someone else in your class and ask them to annotate it, with things that work especially well and things that you might change.
- Show it to a second reader. Ask them to comment on what you've written and on the comments of another reader.
- Write a final version of your poem, to be displayed on your classroom wall. If you can, design it on a computer, choosing a font that will bring out the qualities of what you have written.

Listen Mr. Oxford don
Take something you feel strongly about. Write it in the style of John Agard's poem, using your own dialect or voice.
For instance, you might write: 'Listen Mr. Film Censor' or 'Listen Mr. Dentist' or 'Listen Mr. School teacher'.

Not-Enough-Pocket-Money Blues
This poem works partly because of the patterns it sets up and then breaks in the very last line. Try writing a poem with a similar pattern:
'Could see myself…
But I've got the … blues.'
Decide what your blues are.
Create a compound word to describe them, for instance, the 'Too-Tired-To-Get-Up-In-The-Morning Blues'.

Five Deities
Make up a few more modern deities to add to John Agard's five. Write a verse for each one. For instance, you could write about: the god(dess) of the ice-cream van, the Internet, football, Nintendo, Breakfast TV, rap or the movies.

A Hello from Cello
Try writing a poem in the shape of another object, for instance, a tennis racquet, a question mark, a piece of cutlery or a living creature.

Crybaby Prime Minister
Try writing a poem, where you imagine an ideal (but unlikely!) person. For instance, your poem could start:
'I'd love to be taught by a werewolf teacher' or 'I'd love to play music with a tone-deaf musician'.

Hippo Writes a Love Poem to His Wife and **Hippo Writes a Love Poem to Her Husband**
Write love poems for other husband and wife creatures, such as snakes, sloths, butterflies or giraffes.
Like Agard, try inventing words that sound like the creatures you're describing. One way of doing this is to take words in one word class and turn them into another. For example,

Verb	**Adjective**
Slither	*Slitherous*

Poetry Jump-up

Tell me if Ah seeing right
Take a look down de street

Words dancin
words dancin
till dey sweat
words like fishes
jumpin out a net
words wild and free
joinin de poetry revelry
words back to back
words belly to belly

Come on everybody
come and join de poetry band
dis is poetry carnival
dis is poetry bacchanal
when inspiration call
take yu pen in yu hand
if yu don't have a pen
take yu pencil in yu hand
if you don't have a pencil
what the hell
so long de feeling start to swell
just shout de poem out

Words jumpin off de page
tell me if Ah seein right
words like birds
jumpin out a cage
take a look down de street
words shakin dey waist
words shakin dey bum
words wit black skin
words wit white skin
words wit brown skin
words wit no skin at all
words huggin up words
an sayin I want to be a poem today
rhyme or no rhyme
I is a poem today
I mean to have a good time

Words feeling hot hot hot
big words feeling hot hot hot
lil words feeling hot hot hot
even sad word cant help
tappin dey toe
to de riddum of de poetry band

Dis is poetry carnival
dis is poetry bacchanal
so come on everybody
join de celebration
all yu need is plenty perspiration
an a little inspiration
plenty perspiration
an a little inspiration

Rainbow

When you see
de rainbow
you know
God know
wha he doing –
one big smile
across the sky –
I tell you
God got style
the man got style

When you see
raincloud pass
and de rainbow
make a show
I tell you
is God doing
limbo
the man doing
limbo

But sometimes
you know
when I see
de rainbow
so full of glow
and curving
like she bearing child
I does want know
if God
ain't a woman

If that is so
the woman got style
man she got style

A Hello from Cello

Stroke

me

high

Stroke

me

low

with a ripple of your bow

till my plump body

begins to glow

with the O-so-sweet harmony.

Make me hum make me buzz make me drone.

Rest my slender neck beside your own.

Close ƒ me in the secret of ƒ your lap

till fall oƒ curtain and fade oƒ clap.

Remember my ornate toe will be curled

like a rude question mark

against the applause in your ear.

I may even whisper four-letter words

such as

Bach

Aria

Opus

Crybaby Prime Minister

I'd love to be led
by a crybaby prime minister
who'd burst into tears
whenever people bled

I'd love to be led
by a crybaby prime minister
who'd sob and sob
for everyone without a job

I'd love to be led
by a crybaby prime minister
who'd lose all control
when told of old folks in the cold

I'd love to be led
by a crybaby prime minister
who'd whimper for a while
at the mention of nuclear missile

I'd love to be led
by a crybaby prime minister
who'd suddenly weep
for children with nowhere to sleep

I'd love to be led
by a crybaby prime minister
whose eyes would go red
when trees of the forest are felled

Yes, there's something to be said
for a nation being led
by a crybaby prime minister
who'd reach for a hanky
with a lump in the throat

Such a prime minister
might be worth a vote.

Hippo Writes a Love Poem to his Wife

Oh my beautiful fat wife
Larger to me than life
Smile broader than the river Nile
My winsome waddlesome
You do me proud in the shallow of morning
You do me proud in the deep of night
Oh, my bodysome mud-basking companion.

Hippo Writes a Love Poem to her Husband

Oh my lubby-dubby hubby-hippo
With your widely-winning lippo
    My Sumo-thrasher of water
Dearer to me than any two-legger
        How can I live without
Your ponderful potamus pout?

Listen Mr Oxford don

Me not no Oxford don
me a simple immigrant
from Clapham Common
I didn't graduate
I immigrate

But listen Mr Oxford don
I'm a man on de run
and a man on de run
is a dangerous one

I ent have no gun
I ent have no knife
but mugging de Queen's English
is the story of my life

I don't need no axe
to split/   up yu syntax
I don't need no hammer
to mash/   up yu grammar

I warning you Mr Oxford don
I'm a wanted man
and a wanted man
is a dangerous one

Dem accuse me of assault
on de Oxford dictionary/
imagine a concise peaceful man like me/
dem want me serve time
for inciting rhyme to riot
but I tekking it quiet
down here in Clapham Common

I'm not a violent man Mr Oxford don
I only armed wit mih human breath
but human breath
is a dangerous weapon

So mek dem send one big word after me
I ent serving no jail sentence
I slashing suffix in self-defence
I bashing future wit present tense
and if necessary

I making de Queen's English accessory/to
my offence

Not-Enough-Pocket-Money Blues

I could see myself stepping light and slow
in them jeans
so hip-sharp-tight and full-of-flow.
Could just…
But I've got me the no-cash no-dosh
not-enough-pocket-money blues.

Could see myself slinking to school
in them trainers
so jaguar-sleek and puma-cool.
Could just…
But I've got me the no-cash no-dosh
not-enough-pocket-money blues.

Could see myself a fashion queen
in that top
so flirty-smart and snazzy-sleeved.
Could just…
But I've got me the no-cash no-dosh
not-enough-pocket-money blues.

Could see myself all summery
in that hat
so patchwork-wicked and flowery.
Could just…
But I've got me the no-cash no-dosh
not-enough-pocket-money blues.

I guess I can always ask Mum.

Five Deities

1. The god of pimples
is a raspberryeyed
tonguetied schemer.

He sits on an Olympus
of scabs and pustules
surrounded by his eloquent
blotchhead advisers

He awaits the moment
        to ambush
the unsuspecting adolescent.

Then one day when you're smartly
 dressed and feeling cheeky,
 he'll give the move-in orders
 to his army of acne

2. The god of the ghettoblaster
cannot speak a word of Greek
but he surveys the underground
swinging his chariot of sound.

He observes from far the frantic ratrace.
Cares not for the laws of silence
or the formality of a briefcase.

The god of the ghettoblaster
    moves at his own music-driven pace
    sending his highvoltage thunderbolt
    into the eardrums of puny mortals.

3. The goddess of trainers
is a fleetfooted
maker of tracks to far-out and beyond.

She's never heard of high-tech or low-tech.
She strides bedecked
    in the whirlwind
    of her Atalanta steps.

The goddess of trainers
    beckons
        an infinity of directions.

4. The god of the skateboard
    is a surfer
    on road waves

a T-shirt Poseidon
in the Saturday morning centre of town.
Pavements are his kingdom.

    With an up
    and a down
    and a fancy
    wheel around

    Who dares deny him attention?

5. The goddess of the personal stereo
is a ruler of the earhive.
Queen Bee amplified.

And a thousand
funky bees
obey her electronic command.

Soon they will fill the air with a crackling
fuzz
and the goddess of the personal stereo
will glory in the beat of the buzz…the
buzz…

I saw a child

> **In this unit you will learn:**
> - how to read poems in an active and questioning way
> - how poetic language and form contribute to meaning
> - how to make judgements and express viewpoints on texts
> - how to plan and carry out a presentation on a poem you have chosen.

Five Years Old

Being five   Group and whole work

- In small groups, talk about memories of what you were like when you were five years old. You may want to use some of these prompts to spark off ideas:
  - things you were afraid of
  - what made you laugh
  - what made you cry
  - strange or funny ideas you had (for instance, did you believe in fairies?)
  - foods you remember really liking or hating
  - how you got on with brothers or sisters
  - what school was like
  - examples of feeling small.

- Share a few memories as a whole class, then listen to James Tate's poem about being five years old.

Five Years Old

Stars fell all night.
The iceman had been very generous that day
with his chips and slivers.

And I buried my pouch of jewels
inside a stone casket under the porch,
their beauty saved for another world.

And then my sister came home
and I threw a dart through her cheek
and cried all night,

so much did I worship her.

James Tate

What makes poems special is that they often can't be explained quickly and easily. The more you look at them the more there is to see. There isn't just one right answer to the question, 'What's it about?' You are going to spend some time exploring what this poem seems to be about and what makes it special as a poem.

Looking at words and phrases   Pair work

■ Look closely at these words and phrases from the poem. Spend time on each one, thinking about all the associations and ideas they suggest to you. Write them out and annotate them with ideas and questions. One example has been done for you, to give you some ideas.

The iceman — is this a man who comes round with ice? Is it about a time before fridges? Or maybe it's a metaphor for winter — the arrival of cold weather has been personified as a man who brings ice to the houses.

Stars fell all night

The iceman

his chips and slivers

my pouch of jewels

another world

a dart

worship

■ Now look back at the poem and try to summarise your ideas, in a few statements. You could use some of these sentence starters to help you:

The poem seems to be about …
On the other hand, maybe it's about …
One puzzling phrase is …
One thing it might be saying is …
Another possibility is …

■ Share your ideas on what the poem is about in class discussion.

The language of the poem   Group work
The poem uses language in interesting ways, to give a sense of what it's like to be a small child.

■ Look at this list of language features and see if you can find an example of each one in the poem.

- Sentences joined with the connective 'and'
- Simple, short words of just one syllable
- Everyday words
- Special, magical or fairytale words
- Words that an adult would use
- Unusual word order

■ Now see whether you can explain what the effect of each of these features is. You could choose between some of the phrases below to help you.

It sounds like children do when they tell a story, or tell about something that's happened to them.

It gives a sense of a child's voice, using the words a child would use.

It adds a sense of mystery and importance to the event.

It's very spare and simple.

It sounds like an adult remembering past experiences.

■ Pull together all of your ideas about the poem, by writing two statements, as a group, using these sentence starters to help you.

What's especially interesting about the poem is the way that it ....
The phrase we liked best is .... because ....

■ Share your ideas as a whole class, including both your observations on the language features and your group statements about the poem.

Full Moon and Little Frieda

'Full Moon and Little Frieda' is another poem about early childhood.

Before reading the poem   Class work
■ Brainstorm all your ideas about the moon and its associations, both for adults and children. The spidergram below gives you a few ideas to get you started.

the moon seems to look
the man in the moon —— **Moon** *down on us*

■ Share ideas about the title. What does it suggest the poem may be about?

Reading the poem   Individual work
■ Read the whole poem, or listen to it being read aloud to you.

■ Ask questions of the poem and note down your first ideas about it.

Full Moon and Little Frieda

A cool small evening shrunk to a dog bark and the
      clank of a bucket –

And you listening.

A spider's web, tense for the dew's touch.
A pail lifted, still and brimming – mirror
To tempt a first star to a tremor

Cows are going home in the lane there, looping the
      hedges with their warm wreaths of breath –
A dark river of blood, many boulders,
Balancing unspilled milk.

'Moon!' you cry suddenly, 'Moon! Moon!'
The moon has stepped back like an artist gazing
      amazed at a work
That points at him amazed.

Ted Hughes

Taking your ideas further   Group work

■   Share your questions. Talk about your first ideas about the poem.

■   Look at the alternative titles for the poem listed below. Talk about each one,
    deciding how well it captures what the poem is about. Choose the one you think fits
    the poem best.

    – A Special Moment
    – An Experience of Nature
    – The Magic of Childhood
    – Fatherly Love
    – Seeing the World Through a Child's Eyes
    – Admiring Creation
    – A Revelation
    – The Wonder of the World

■   Try to summarise these first responses, in a few statements. Use these sentence
    starters to help you:

The most puzzling lines are …
One thing they might be saying is …
Another possibility is …
The poem seems to be about …
What's especially interesting about the poem is the way that it …
The phrase we liked best is … because …

Discussion on the poem   Class work

■ Listen to each other's ideas about the meanings in the poem, which lines you liked and why.

Digging deeper – a close focus on language   Group and class work

■ Look again at the opening to the poem.

> A cool small evening shrunk to a dog bark and the
> clank of a bucket –
>
> And you listening.
>
> A spider's web, tense for the dew's touch.
> A pail lifted, still and brimming – mirror
> To tempt a first star to a tremor

Poetry has been described as 'language made strange'.

■ In small groups, talk about what is 'strange' or particularly special about the language in the opening of the poem. Each group should focus on *one* of the aspects of language listed below. (Use everyday language to describe what you notice, if you don't know the precise terms. For instance, you might say, 'Not all the normal bits of the verbs are there – 'has' and 'are' are missing.' Another way of saying this is that the 'auxiliary verbs' are missing.) Go on to talk about what effect this has.

Layout
- What choices has the poet made about where to start a new line?
- Are there any spaces between lines? Why?
- What do you notice about the length of the lines?

Sound
- In what ways is alliteration used (repeated consonant sounds, usually at the beginning of words)? What's the effect?
- In what ways is assonance used (repeated vowel sounds)? What's the effect?
- In what ways is onomatopoeia used (the sound is like the thing described)? What's the effect?
- Do you notice anything about the rhythm (sometimes described as the beat, or the way syllables are stressed, when it is read aloud)?

Grammar
- What's interesting about the way verbs are used?
- What can you tell about tenses of the verbs?
- What do you notice about the adjectives?
- What do you notice about the use of personal pronouns ('I', 'we', 'you', ' he', 'she', 'it', 'they')?

■ Report back your group's ideas to the rest of the class.

A poetry writing experiment Homework

■ Write a short paragraph, of no more than five sentences, describing a moment from the past that has stayed in your memory. It might be the way things looked, or felt, tastes, or sounds that you remember most powerfully. These are some suggestions for the kinds of things you might write about:
  - a nightmare
  - witnessing or taking part in an argument or fight
  - opening an amazing present
  - the experience of Christmas when you were younger
  - being terrified at night.

■ Now use what you have learnt about the special features of poetry to turn your paragraph into the first two or three lines of a poem. Make lots of changes to words before you finally decide on a version you like. Make sure that your piece of paper has several crossings out and changes and *don't* copy it out into best – it will be interesting for other people to see all the changes you made before arriving at your final version!

Reading a range of poems on children and parents

A quick recap Class work

■ Read aloud some of the paragraphs and first lines you worked on independently.

■ Identify anything you liked about the way other people turned their ideas into poetry. Collect interesting lines and phrases to display in the classroom.

First impressions Group work

■ Take turns in reading aloud each of the poems on pages 51-55.

■ After each poem has been read, pause for a few moments to think about it and pick out any of the headings below that describe your immediate responses to it.

Puzzling   Appealing   Funny   Challenging   Entertaining

Lively   Beautiful   Difficult   Powerful

Clever   Moving

A sorting activity   Group work

■   Skim through the poems again. This time try to sort them in different ways, making some connections and contrasts between the poems.

> Comic poems
> Serious poems
> Modern poems
> Pre-twentieth century poems
> Poems with an adult voice
> Poems with a child's voice
> Poems addressed *to* a child
> Poems about what childhood is like
> Poems where the look on the page is especially interesting
> Poems where the sound is especially important

Whole class discussion   Class work

■   Share your ideas on the sorting activity.

■   Talk about your first impressions of this collection of poems.

Poems for an anthology   Homework

■   From the collection choose one poem that you think would be suitable for each of these sections of a new poetry anthology.

Breaking the Rules
Looking Back
Strong Voices
Life and Death
Growing Up

■   List all of your reasons for your choices, so that you can explain your decisions to the rest of the class.

Digging deeper – what's special about a poem?

A quick recap   Class work

■   Listen to different people presenting their reasons for choosing poems for different sections of an anthology. Discuss differences of viewpoint.

Poems and descriptions – a matching game   Pair and class work

■   Match the description on the next page to the poem you think it refers to.

It's addressed to a child. It is a short poem, structured by a simple pattern of repeated lines. This simplicity and directness helps to suggest the power of the narrator's feelings for the child. There is a change in the pattern in the third line from the end of the poem, emphasising the heart-breaking situation for the narrator.

■   Share your decisions.

Writing descriptions

■   Write similar descriptions for two or three of the other poems. Avoid saying the *most* obvious things, like the name of the poem or poet, but make sure you give enough description to pin down what's special about it. Use the description above as a model to help you.

Matching poems

■   Take turns to read aloud one of your descriptions. See if the class can match it to the right poem. If they can't, work as a class to re-draft the description to match the poem more closely.

Presenting a poem

You are going to do a presentation on one of the poems in the collection 'I saw a child', either for your class or for a year assembly.

What makes a good presentation?   Class work

■   Share ideas about what would make a presentation on a poem interesting and enjoyable for other people of your age. You might think about issues such as:
   - what the presentation might consist of
   - how it could be made lively and varied
   - how eye contact, body language, gestures and movement might contribute
   - what visual aids or sound effects you could use
   - how to time and pace the presentation
   - how to go about planning it.

Choosing one poem   Group work

■   Choose which poem you want to present.

■   Talk about the poem, following the strategies you used when looking at 'Full Moon and Little Frieda' (questioning, taking notes, looking closely at language and so on).

■   Plan your presentation on your poem. Your presentation could include ideas suggested in the whole class discussion, as well as any of the ideas listed on the next page.

- A reading or performance of the poem (possibly with more than one voice).
- An introduction to the poem or commentary after the reading.
- A role-play on the situation of the poem.
- A few images to go with the poems (from magazines, books, postcards and so on).
- A piece of music to introduce or end your presentation.

Doing the presentations Class work

■ Present your poems, in an assembly, to the whole class, or to one or two other groups, depending on the time available. While other presentations are happening, jot down a few brief notes on anything that worked particularly well, or any ideas you have for improvements.

Talking about the presentations

■ Share anything that you particularly liked about other people's presentations and talk about what features these demonstrated. For instance, if you say that one group's presentation was very lively, try to explain what features made it lively. Was it the fact that everyone was involved in speaking? Did they vary their tone of voice? Did they have short sections, following on from one another, without too many pauses?

Evaluating your presentation Homework

■ Write a short personal evaluation of your group's presentation, focusing both on your role in it and on the final performance. Reflect on the ideas raised in the class discussion.

Further activities

Writing creatively – a poem Individual work

■ Write a poem of your own, based on one of the poems in the collection. The examples below might give you some ideas as a starting-point.

Five years old A poem about the misunderstandings and ways of seeing things that you can remember from early childhood	**Gust Becos I Cud Not Spel** Another revenge poem titled 'Just Because I Could Not …'
Spring and Fall Margaret's reply to the poet	**Bits of Early Days** A poem about *your* childhood starting alternate verses with 'Still a shock to remember' and 'Still a joy to remember'

Writing critically – a response to the poems on childhood

■ Choose one poem to write about, exploring what's interesting or special about it and what you particularly liked.

■ Choose two or three poems to compare. Pick poems that have lots of differences as well as similarities, to give you plenty to write about.

Traditional African Lullaby

Someone would like to have you as her child
But you are mine.
Someone would like to rear you on a costly mat
But you are mine.
Someone would like to place you on a camel blanket
But you are mine.
I have you to rear on a torn old mat,
Someone would like to have you as her child
But you are mine.

Akan woman

On My First Son

Farewell, thou child of my right hand, and joy;
    My sin was too much hope of thee, loved boy.
Seven years thou wert lent to me, and I thee pay,
    Exacted by thy fate, on the just day.

Oh, could I lose all father now! For why
    Will man lament the state he should envy?
To have so soon 'scaped world's and flesh's rage,
    And, if no other misery, yet age?
Rest in soft peace, and, asked, say here doth lie
    Ben Jonson his best piece of poetry;
For whose sake, henceforth, all his vows be such,
    As what he loves may never like too much.

Ben Jonson (1572-1637)

Gust Becos I Cud Not Spel

Gust becos I cud not spel
It did not mean I was daft
When the boys in school red my riting
Some of them laffed.

But now I am the dictater
They have to rite like me
Utherwise they cannot pas
Ther GCSE

Some of the girls wer ok
But those who laffed a lot
Have al bean rownded up
And hav recintly bean shot

The teecher who corrected my speling
As not been shot at al
But four the last fifteen howers
As bean standing up against a wal

He has to stand ther until he can spel
Figgymisgrugifooniyn the rite way
I think he will stand ther forever
I just inventid it today.

Brian Patten

Spring and Fall

to a young child
Margaret, are you grieving
Over Goldengrove unleaving?
Leaves, like the things of man, you
With your fresh thoughts care for, can you?
Ah! as the heart grows older
It will come to such sights colder
By and by, nor spare a sigh
Though worlds of wanwood leafmeal lie;
And yet you will weep and know why
Now no matter, child, the name:
Sorrow's springs are the same.
Nor mouth had, no nor mind, expressed
What heart heard of, ghost guessed:
It is the blight man was born for,
It is Margaret you mourn for.

Gerard Manley Hopkins
(1844-89)

I Saw a Child

I saw a child with silver hair.
Stick with me and I'll take you there.
   Clutch my hand.
   Don't let go.
The fields are mined and the wind blows cold.
The wind blows through his silver hair.

The Blue Vein River is broad and deep.
The branches creak and the shadows leap.
   Clutch my hand.
   Stick to the path.
The fields are mined and the moon is bright.
I saw a child who will never sleep.

Far from the wisdom of the brain
I saw a child grow old in pain.
   Clutch my hand.
   Stay with me.
The fields are mined by the enemy.
Tell me we may be friends again.

Far from the wisdom of the blood
I saw a child reach from the mud.
   Clutch my hand.
   Clutch my heart.
The fields are mined and the moon is dark.
The Blue Vein River is in full flood.

Far from the wisdom of the heart
I saw a child being torn apart.
   Is this you?
   Is this me?
The fields are mined and the night is long.
Stick with me when the shooting starts.

James Fenton

On Turning Ten

The whole idea of it makes me feel
like I'm coming down with something,
something worse than any stomach ache
or the headaches I get from reading in bad light –
a kind of measles of the spirit,
a mumps of the psyche,
a disfiguring chicken pox of the soul.

You tell me it is too early to be looking back,
but that is because you have forgotten
the perfect simplicity of being one
and the beautiful complexity introduced by two.
But I can lie on my bed and remember every digit.
At four I was an Arabian wizard.
I could make myself invisible
by drinking a glass of milk a certain way.
At seven I was a soldier, at nine a prince.

But now I am mostly at the window
watching the late afternoon light.
Back then it never fell so solemnly
against the side of my tree house,
and my bicycle never leaned against the garage
as it does today,
all the dark blue speed drained out of it.

This is the beginning of sadness, I say to myself,
as I walk through the universe in my sneakers.
It is time to say good-bye to my imaginary friends,
time to turn the first big number.
It seems only yesterday I used to believe
there was nothing under my skin but light.
If you cut me I would shine.
But now when I fall upon the sidewalks of life,
I skin my knees. I bleed.

Billy Collins

Bits of Early Days

Still a shock to remember
facing that attacking
dog's fangs and eyes at its gate.
Seeing our slug-eating dog come in
the house, mouth gummed up, plastered.

Still a joy to remember
standing at our palm-fringed beach
watching sunrise streak the sea.
Finding a hen's nest in high grass
full of eggs.
Galloping a horse barebacked
over the village pasture.

Still a shock to remember
eating with fingers and caught
oily handed by my teacher.
Seeing a dog like goat-hide flattened
there in the road.

Still a joy to remember
myself a small boy milking a cow
in new sunlight.
Smelling asafoetida on
a village baby I held.
Sucking fresh honey from its comb
just robbed.

Still a shock to remember
watching weighted kittens tossed in
the sea's white breakers.
Seeing our village stream dried up
with rocks exposed
like dry guts and brains.

Still a joy to remember
walking barefoot on a bed of dry leaves
there in deep woods.
Finding my goat with all of three
new wobbly kids.

Still a shock to remember
facing that youth-gang attack and all
the needless abuse.
Holding my first identity card
stamped 'Negro'.

Still a joy to remember
walking fourteen miles from four a.m.
into town market.
Surrounded by sounds of church-bell
in sunlight and birdsong.

James Berry

Childhood

I used to think that grown-up people chose
To have stiff backs and wrinkles round their nose,
And veins like small fat snakes on either hand,
On purpose to be grand.
Till through the banisters I watched one day
My great-aunt Etty's friend who was going away,
And how her onyx beads had come unstrung.
I saw her grope to find them as they rolled;
And then I knew that she was helplessly old,
As I was helplessly young.

Frances Cornford

The Adventures of Carla Johnson

She always says, night then love I'll leave
your door open. I always sneak out of bed and close it.
Every step I take has to be as quiet as held-in breath.
I cannot afford a pin dropping, the shock of a sneeze.
So when I close the door, it takes me half an hour
to make it from my bed and back again.
So slow to avoid the cat's miaow of the door,
then it's tiptoe over the threadbare carpet.

When it's dark in my room my friend
Carla Johnson comes – she has wings
fabulous things, kiwi fruit and tangerines.
Come on Carla, she taps me on the shoulder.
We fly out the window, quiet as burglars.

We only fly to places with good names
that begin with the same letter of the alphabet.
On a single night we covered Alaska, Alabama
Albania; tonight is Louisiana Lithuania and Largs
because I went there when I was four
(strictly speaking, it is not a nice name).
Far from being tired in the morning
I feel quite rejuvenated – no jet lag whatsoever.

Jackie Kay

Pairing poems

In this unit you will learn:
- how different poets treat the same subjects and themes
- how poets create meaning and mood through language
- about the choices poets make and their effects
- how to use small group talk, to expand your ideas and summarise key points, ready for reporting back to the class
- how to write a comparison of two poems
- how to use published poems as a springboard for your own poetry writing.

Representing a poem

A drawing game   Pair work

You will be given one poem by your teacher. You will be doing a quick sketch, as a way of getting to know the poem and thinking about its mood and style as well as its subject and themes. First, look at how someone else has represented a poem visually.

■   Look at this postcard, in which the artist, Kate Owens has created a visual image to go with a poem. How has she tried to capture:
- the subject of the poem
- the mood of the poem
- the style of the poem?

Think, for example, about the way she has used shade and tone as well as the actual image she has chosen.

BUFFALO BILL

Buffalo Bill's
defunct
          who used to
          ride a watersmooth-silver
                    stallion
and break onetwothreefourfive pigeonsjustlikethat
                    Jesus

he was a handsome man
          and what i want to know is
how do you like your blueeyed boy
Mister Death

E.E.Cummings

■ Here is one person's analysis of the postcard as a way of representing the painting. Talk about what it says and how far you agree with it.

> In the painting which accompanies e.e.cummings' poem 'Buffalo Bill', the central image looks like a cowboy, the most famous example of which was 'Buffalo Bill'. This means it helps conjure up the associations of the Wild West, such as daring, bravery, heroism. However, in the poem the final line reveals that 'Death' has conquered even the famous cowboy 'Buffalo Bill'. The fact that in the painting the cowboy image is turned away from the viewer and is fading into the background combined with the dark and rather threatening colours capture this idea in the poem.

A picture of your poem   Pair work

■ Now read the poem you have been given, out loud. Read it a second time. Talk about what kind of painting or drawing you might do to represent it.

- What would the colours and tones be like?
- What would be in the foreground, middle and background?
- What would be the main focus? What would the viewer's eye be drawn to?
- Would it try to tell the story of the poem or capture the mood?
- What style would it be? (For instance, could it be painted in oil with sweeping brushstrokes? Or would delicate watercolours be more appropriate? What about a collage?)

■ Do a quick sketch, with annotations, to represent your poem.

■ Join up with another pair who have looked at the same poem as you. Compare your ideas for representing the poem visually.

■ Your ideas for images should have helped you to begin to think about the poem. Now talk about the poem in more detail, jotting down a few key words and phrases to remind you of your ideas. Use the prompts below to help you.

- What is the poem about?
- What is its mood?
- How does it begin?
- How does it develop? (Are there any shifts? Does the ending change things?)
- What's the voice of the poem? (What tone? Who's it talking to?)
- What are the most interesting choices of language and style? (You should think about vocabulary, use of rhyme and rhythm, use of layout, use of sound and so on.)

Comparing poems   Group and class work

Each poet has his or her own voice. Each poem takes an individual angle on a subject. Comparing poems on the same theme can help to highlight what's *special* about each one. Work in your original pairs. You will be joining up with another pair, working on a poem that has some similarities with yours but some differences. You will be presenting your poems to each other and comparing them.

■ Join up with a pair who have the poem that is matched with yours. Present your poems to each other, using both your sketches and your discussion notes.

■ Talk about the similarities and differences between your poems. Your aim, as a four, is to make a list of the *six* most important and interesting similarities and differences between the two poems.

■ Feed back to the whole class, comparing your list of ideas with those of other groups reading the same poems.

Reading pupil writing
■ Read this piece of writing by a KS3 pupil, comparing two of the poems in this unit.

'Exodus' and 'Children in Wartime'

Both poems are about wartime. The theme of the first poem is the war in Kosovo, away from all the soldiers and fighting, where the normal people are suffering under the effects of the war and are packing their belongings, getting ready to leave. It is written in the present tense. The theme of the second poem is different. It is probably one of the world wars as it talks about sirens and shelters, which are common more in the Second World War than the first. The author compares the effects of the war with things like a storm. This helps to give the poem atmosphere but says that these things are much, much worse than a storm could ever be. It is written in the past tense.

When the poems describe people's feelings they portray them in different ways. In the first poem the author speaks about crying babies and hobbling grandmothers who have kept the grief locked up tight away until now, when they see the desolation in the war-stricken land they once called their home. The most upsetting thing is near the end where the poem says, 'the ditches filled with blood and suitcases' which means that some of the people leaving never made it out. Also the part that says, 'abandoned toys dragging a severed limb/a three legged dog limps off across the plain' is sad as the most innocent things are injured, abandoned and forgotten in the panic. By contrast, in the second poem it doesn't talk as much about people's feelings but more about what things were changing around her and comparing them to everyday things like storms and people playing bowls and the starry sky at night, when the war is obviously not an everyday thing.

Both poems are similar in the way that both talk about the physical changes in the surroundings. In the second poem it says about 'thunder left such huge craters of silence' and in the first it says, 'Earth's thunderous surface' which gives the impression of big physical changes. They are also similar in the way that they talk about the death of animals and people a lot.

Though both poems are similar in these ways they also have a number of important differences. In poem 1 it has no capital letters whereas in poem 2 it does. This may only be a small difference but it completely changed my whole understanding of the poems. Also in poem one it doesn't have one sentence on one line, like it continues onto the next line, so you have to work out for yourself where to take a breath and where a pause would sound appropriate but in poem 2 it has lines that sound fine if you pause at the end and capital letters where you can take quite a big breath so it is a lot easier to understand and read aloud the first time you see it.

Another difference is that poem 1 is written as if the author was writing whilst walking around looking at the despair in people's faces and poem 2 is written as if the author was remembering what it was like. In other words poems 1 is written in the present tense and poem 2 is written in the past tense.

Of the two poems I found poem 2 the most interesting as it would be almost jolly if it wasn't such an upsetting subject. I also found it the easiest to understand as it has a simple structure, whereas poem 2 doesn't.

■   Look closely at the way it is written, using the prompts given here.

- Identify all the words that help you to follow the structure of the ideas (for instance, 'whereas', 'by contrast' and so on).
- How are the points structured to make the comparison?
- Does it give evidence from the poems to back up the points made?
- Does it give you new ideas and insights into the poems?

Writing about two poems   Individual work

■   Choose a pairing to write about yourself. You could write about the poems you jigsawed, or another pair from this unit. Think about all the strategies you discussed for structuring a comparison, including:
- using words that signal the comparison (such as 'whereas...' and 'while')
- writing about similarities and differences, rather than writing first about one poem then writing about the next
- using evidence from the text
- analysing what's *special* about each poem
- thinking about the choices the poets have made.

You could use the structure suggested here to help you.

Both poems are about …

The theme of the first poem is …

The theme of the second poem is different. It…

Both poems are similar in the way that they …

They are also similar in their way of …

Though both poems are similar in these ways, they also have a number of important differences. Whereas poem 1 …, poem 2 … For instance …

While poem 1…, poem 2 …This is shown when …

Of the two poems, the one I found most interesting was……. I liked the way the poet….

Writing your own poem

Finding a starting-point   Individual work

■   Use one of the ideas in the box on page 60 to help you write a poem of your own. (You could try starting more than one idea, then develop the one that works best.)

Choose one line from any of the poems in this unit, as the first line of a poem of your own.	Write another stanza for one of the poems, or a prequel or sequel to the poem.
Choose one of the titles and write a poem that offers a completely different angle to that of the original. For instance, 'To a goose', might be a love poem written by its mate, 'The Sheepdog' might be a sheep's perspective on that dog, or 'Poem' might be the daughter or mother's view of the man.	Borrow the structure of one of the poems and put your own subject into it. Below is an example of part of 'This Moment', transformed in this way. (Notice how it mostly uses the same word classes and each line often has the same number of syllables.)

A neighbourhood.
At dusk.

Things are getting ready
to happen
out of sight.

Stars and moths.
And rinds slanting around fruit.

A tournament.
At ten.

Legs are getting ready
To run
Lean of limb.

Boots and socks.
And nerves trembling about results.

Glasgow 5 March 1971

With a ragged diamond
of shattered plate-glass
a young man and his girl
are falling backwards into a shop-
window.
The young man's face
is bristling with fragments of glass
and the girl's leg has caught
on the broken window
and spurts arterial blood
over her wet-look white coat.
Their arms are starfished out
braced for impact,
their faces show surprise, shock,
and the beginning of pain.
The two youths who have pushed them
are about to complete the operation
reaching into the window
to loot what they can smartly.
Their faces show no expression.
It is a sharp clear night
in Sauchiehall Street.
In the background two drivers
keep their eyes on the road.

Edwin Morgan

This moment

A neighbourhood.
At dusk.

Things are getting ready
to happen
out of sight.

Stars and moths.
And rinds slanting around fruit.

But not yet.

One tree is black.
One window is yellow as butter.

A woman leans down to catch a child
who has run into her arms
this moment.

Stars rise.
Moths flutter.
Apples sweeten in the dark.

Eavan Boland

Exodus

In such a time as this when multitudes
stream out abandoned bombed from ruined cities
grandmothers hobbling babies bicycles
luggage on carts and backs the crying children
there are no boundaries a private grief
shrinks to a pin prick on this frontier
the ditches filled with blood and suitcases
lovers shot through the heart abandoned toys
dragging a severed limb
a three legged dog limps off across the plain

this unmourned multitude who trudge
across earth's thunderous surface
Belgrade to Kosovo to Baghdad burning.

Dorothy Hewett

Children in Wartime

Sirens ripped open
the warm silk of sleep;
we ricocheted to the shelter
moated by streets
that ran with darkness.
People said it was a storm,
but flak
had not the right sound
for rain;
thunder left such huge craters
of silence,
we knew this was no giant
playing bowls.
And later,
when I saw the jaw of glass,
where once had hung
my window spun with stars;
it seemed the sky
lay broken on my floor.

Isobel Thrilling

Poem

And if it snowed and snow covered the drive
he took a spade and tossed it to one side.
And always tucked his daughter up at night.
And slippered her the one time that she lied.

And every week he tipped up half his wage.
And what he didn't spend each week he saved.
And praised his wife for every meal she made.
And once, for laughing, punched her in the face.

And for his mum he hired a private nurse.
And every Sunday taxied her to church.
And he blubbed when she went from bad to worse.
And twice he lifted ten quid from her purse.

Here's how they rated him when they looked back:
sometimes he did this, sometimes he did that.

Simon Armitage

Who's Who

A shilling life will give you all the facts:
How Father beat him, how he ran away,
What were the struggles of his youth, what acts
Made him the greatest figure of his day:
Of how he fought, fished, hunted, worked all night,
Though giddy, climbed new mountains; named a
sea:
Some of the last researchers even write
Love made him weep his pints like you and me.

With all his honours on, he sighed for one
Who, say astonished critics, lived at home;
Did little jobs about the house with skill
And nothing else; could whistle; would sit still
Or potter round the garden; answered some
Of his long marvellous letters but kept none.

W.H. Auden

The Sheepdog

After the very bright light
And the talking bird,
And the singing,
And the sky filled up wi' wings,
And then the silence,

Our lads sez
We'd better go, then.
Stay, Shep. Good dog, stay.
So I stayed wi' t' sheep.

After they cum back,
It sounded grand, what they'd seen:
Camels, and kings, and such,
Wi' presents – human sort,
Not the kind you eat –
And a baby. Presents wes for him.
Our lads took him a lamb.

I had to stay behind wi' t' sheep.
Pity they didn't tek me along too.
I'm good wi' lambs,
And the baby might have liked a
dog
After all that myrrh and such.

U.A. Fanthorpe

To a Goose

If thou didst feed on western plains of yore
Or waddle wide with flat and flabby feet
Over some Cambrian mountain's plashy moor,
Or find in farmer's yard a safe retreat
From gipsy thieves and foxes sly and fleet;
If thy grey quills by lawyer guided, trace
Deeds big with ruin to some wretched race,
Or love-sick poet's sonnet, sad and sweet,
Wailing the rigour of some lady fair;
Or if, the drudge of housemaid's daily toil,
Cobwebs and dust thy pinion white besoil,
Departed goose! I neither know nor care.
But this I know, that thou wert very fine
Seasoned with sage and onions and port wine.

Robert Southey

Comparing poems

Songs and words

In this unit you will:
- explore a range of song lyrics and think about the way they work
- focus closely on one song by Travis and its promotional video, to explore the relationship between music, words and visual images
- write song lyrics of your own, in different styles.

Introduction

Write your own pop song   Group work
- Look at these words from a recent pop song.

Never Get Over You

Boy, should've have known it from the start,
You'd go and break my heart,
But I was hoping, praying,
You, you always thought you were right,
But you couldn't see the light,
The truth was shining,
For all the world to see,
You made a fool of me (out of me)
Why did you have to leave

Steps

- How quickly can you write something similar, as a group? Try to come up with a verse for a song in no more than five minutes, using this as your first line:

  If you only knew, just how much I care

- Talk about how easy or difficult this was and why.

Reading and writing lyrics

■ Talk about what you think of the lyrics you first read and your own ones, choosing between the words and phrases below to help you express your opinion.

soppy and sentimental   empty   profound and important

poetic   beautiful   cheap and trashy   clichéd   striking

boring   predictable   memorable   strong   emotional

soulful   powerful   passionate   thought-provoking

■ Look at these titles for pop, rock and jazz songs. Talk about what the titles reveal about what the song will be about and how interesting, unusual or profound the song itself is likely to be.

Heard it Through the Grapevine
Imagine
Strange Fruit
One for Sorrow
Oliver's Army
Road Rage
My Heart will Go On
Hit me Baby One More Time
This Old Heart of Mine
The Lonesome Death of Hattie Carroll

Songs – the new poetry?   Pair work

■ Talk about the following comments about song lyrics. For each one, talk about what it seems to be saying and whether you agree or disagree. Find evidence from your own knowledge of popular music and of poetry to back up your views.

One of the reasons that kids' interest in poetry becomes dulled is that by the time they are in their teens they have got heavily into music. But rap music, for instance, is deeply poetic. It goes back to the oral traditions which poetry first came from.'

William Sieghart, initiator of National Poetry Day

'I think there's a groundswell of people moving towards real songwriters instead of pre-prackaged, production-driven artists.'

Tony Moore, the Kashmir Klub

Reading and writing lyrics

> 'There is poetry in the modern pop/rock album, but not much, and that's how things should be. Songs, I believe, should be clever but simple, because the music that comes with them has an aural significance that is too complex to understand.'

Poems and songs   Class work

The very fact that people talk about some song words being like poems suggests that normally we think of lyrics and poems as different types of writing. When people talk about a song being as good as, or almost as good as a poem, it suggests that lyrics are usually considered to be inferior. So what makes the words of a song different from those of a poem? And do they share any features?

■   Talk about what you think makes lyrics different from poetry and why. Debate whether these differences are hard and fast. Do poems and sones also share some features? For instance, you might want to say that songs have repeated words, phrases or refrains, for listeners to latch onto – but the same is true for many poems, in particular ballads and nursery rhymes. Perhaps you could decide that *all* songs have some element of repetition, while poems don't *have* to use this technique.

Lyrics that count   Pair and class work

'As for the lyrics of the great songs; you cannot hear them without the tune. Saying them over you see they need their music. Lyrics plus music can do what a poem does. That does not make the lyrics a poem. They have ingredients and goals in common. But a cake has an omelette's ingredients. Neither is better; why compare?'

From 'Don't give up the day job, Sir Paul', Ruth Padel, **The Independent**, 16th March 2001, reviewing *Blackbird Singing: Poems and Lyrics 1965-1999* by Paul McCartney, edited by Adrian Mitchell.

So can song lyrics be poetry? Here are some quotations from songs which made the top ten in the UK at the end of the twentieth and beginning of the twenty-first century.

■   Read the lyrics aloud.

1. I sit and wait
Does an angel
Contemplate my fate
And do they know
The places where we go
When we're grey and old
Cause I have been told
That salvation
Lets their wings unfold
So when I'm lying in my bed
Thoughts running through my head
And I feel that love is dead
I'm loving angels instead.

Robbie Williams

2. That's me in the corner
That's me in the spotlight
Losing my religion
Trying to keep up with you
And I don't know if I can do it
Oh no, I've said too much
I haven't said enough
I thought that I heard you laughing
I thought I heard you sing
I think I thought I saw you try

REM

3. If all you've got to do today is find peace of mind
Come round
You can take a piece of mine
If all you've got to do today is hesitate
Come here, you can leave it late with me

If all you've got to do to prove today is your innocence
Calm down, you're as guilty as can be
If all you've got to lose alludes to yesterday

Yesterday's through
Now do anything you please

Space age, road rage, fast lane, minimum wage
Home late, upgrade, short-changed, golden age
Front page, lose face, handmade, space ache
Backstage, outrage, disgraced, maximum weight

Catatonia

4. 'All I wanna do is have a little fun before I die.'
Says the man next to me out of nowhere
It's apropos of nothing
He says his name is William but I'm sure
He's Bill or Billy or Mac or Buddy
And he's plain ugly to me
And I wonder if he's ever had a day of fun in his whole life
We are drinking beer at noon on Tuesday
In a bar that faces a giant car wash
The good people of the world are washing their cars
On their lunch break, hosing and scrubbing as best they can in skirts in suits
They drive their shiny Datsuns and Buicks
Back to the phone company, the record store too

Sheryl Crow

5. She's taking her time making up the reasons
To justify all the hurt inside
Guess she knows from the smiles and the look in their eyes
Everyone's got a theory about the bitter one
They're saying
Mama never loved her much
And daddy never keeps in touch
That's why she never shies away from human affection
But somewhere in a private place
She packs her bags for outer space
And now she's waiting for the right kind of pilot
To come

Savage Garden

Reading and writing lyrics

6. We've come a long long way together
Through the hard times and the good
I have to celebrate you baby
I have to praise you like I should

I have to praise you

I have to praise you like I should
I have to praise you

Fatboy Slim

7. Tender is the night
Lying by your side
Tender is the touch
Of someone that you love too much
Tender is the day
The demons go away
Lord I need to find
Someone who can heal my mind

Blur

8. Sunday all the lights of London
Shining. Sky is fading red to blue
I'm kicking through the Autumn leaves
And wondering where it is you might be going to
Turning back for home
You know I'm feeling so alone
I can't believe
Climbing on the stair
I turn around to see you smiling there
In front of me

David Gray

9. And I'm thinking what a mess we're in
Hard to know where to begin
If I could slip the sickly ties that earthly man has made
And now every mother, can choose the colour of her child
That's not nature's way
Well that's what they said yesterday
There's nothing left to do but pray
I think it's time I found a new religion.

Jamiroquai

10. Seems like yesterday we used to rock the show
I lace the track you lock the flow
So far from hanging on the block of dough
Notorious they got to know that
Life ain't always what it seems to be
Words can't express what you mean to me
And though you're gone
We still a team
Through your family I'll fulfill your dreams.

Puff Daddy

■ Below is a list of some of the features you might expect to find in poetry. Add any more features you can think of. Then talk about which of these features you find in any of the lyrics printed here.

- Rhyme
- Verses
- Condensed language
- Condensed ideas
- Repeated patterns of language, such as refrains or repeated words
- Sound effects contributing to the meaning (alliteration, assonance, onomatopoeia and so on)
- Images – metaphors or similes

■ Briefly talk about whether or not you consider that these are poems in their own right as well as the words of a song. What features do they share with poems? What makes them different from a poem? Make a note of the reasons for your decisions.

■ Take each lyric in turn and vote as a class. Does the presence of these features (for example, rhyme and rhythm) mean the lyric is also a poem? Or does there need to be something more?

■ See if you can agree a set of criteria for what makes a 'poem-lyric', in other words lyrics that are also poems.

Exploring a text

Reading a text – what is it?   Group and class work
■ Read the text on page 69 out loud once and talk about your first responses to it.

■ Share a few readings as a whole class and feed back your ideas about what sort of text it is, using the ideas you've developed from the work you've done so far. Is it a poem or is it a song? How do you know? Think about:
- the structure – the way it is divided up into different sections, for example verse, chorus and bridge (or connecting section)
- the language
- the way the ideas do or do not develop.

■ Look again at the list of features of a poem above and see how many of them you notice in the text.

Everything is open
nothing is set in stone
rivers turn to Ocean
oceans tide you home
home is where the heart is
but your heart had to roam
drifting over bridges
never to return
watching bridges burn

you're driftwood floating underwater
breaking into pieces, pieces, pieces
just driftwood hollow and of no use
waterfalls will find you, bind you,
grind you

nobody is an island
everyone has to go
pillars turn to butter
butterflying low
low is where your heart is
but your heart has to grow
drifting under bridges
never with the flow

and you really didn't think it would
happen

but it really is the end of the line
so I'm sorry that you turned to driftwood
but you've been drifting for a long, long
time
everywhere there's trouble
nowhere safe to go
pushes turn to shovels
shovelling the snow
frozen you have chosen
the path you wish to go
drifting now forever
and forever more
until you reach your shore

you're driftwood floating underwater
breaking into pieces, pieces, pieces
just driftwood hollow and of no use
waterfalls will find you, bind you,
grind you
and you really didn't think it would
happen
but it really is the end of the line
so I'm sorry that you turned to driftwood
but you've been drifting for a long, long
time
you've been drifting for a long, long time
you've been drifting for a long, long time
drifting for a long, long time

Your teacher will tell you what the text is.

What's it about?   Pair Work

■   Talk about the words of 'Driftwood' and what you think they mean. Use the prompts
below to help structure your discussion.

- Talk about the title. What is driftwood? What could it be used as a metaphor for?
- What are your first ideas about the meaning of the song? What kinds of ideas or
feelings is it expressing?
- Pull out all of the nouns and list them on a sheet of paper. What patterns do you
notice? What do they make you think of or feel?
- Pull out all of the verbs, or verb phrases (such as 'is open'). What patterns do you
notice?
- Now you've had a chance to look at the patterns, talk again about what you think
the song is about. Has this close look at patterns helped you?

■   Do you think the words stand up on their own, without the music? Do you think they
work as poetry? Talk about the reasons for your view.

Reading and writing lyrics

Watching 'Driftwood'   Class viewing

Although you might decide that the lyrics stand up in their own right, they were written to be sung. The music adds a layer to the meaning of the song. A further layer of meaning is added by the video produced by the group.

■　　Watch the video for the first time with the sound turned down.

■　　Talk about what seems to be going on and how it relates to the lyrics on the page.

■　　Now watch it a second time, this time listening to the song as well.

■　　What is the connection? Is there a connection? Is the video part of the meaning of the song? Make a note of your first ideas.

■　　Does the video change your understanding of the song? Does it give you any further insights into the meaning of the lyrics? Use the statements below to help you think about, and express your own ideas about the connection between the video, the lyrics and the music.

There is no connection between this song and the video at all. It is just a vehicle for the group.	The video makes you think more carefully about the lyrics of the song. You start to wonder what they might mean, not just what they sound like.	It seems to me that the video shows the group drifting along in their jobs without thinking, just like the song says.	The video doesn't tie down the lyrics and music to a single meaning.

It could mean that the 'You' of the song ('You're driftwood') refers to the girls. They don't look like they're thinking about anything. On the other hand, this suggests they are carefree, whereas the music is quite melancholy.

Sounds and words

The sound of a song – the music – is, of course, a crucial part of the meaning. However, as the lyrics to 'Driftwood' reveal, the sound of the lyrics is also important.

■　　Read the lyrics aloud and make a note of anything which you think is particularly noticeable about the sound of the words.

A great poet of our times?

Reading a controversial writer   Group work

■ Look at these extracts from an article from *The Guardian*, by Giles Foden, the deputy literary editor:

'A brilliant poet'

'The irony in these lines is delicious'

'[it has] all the depth and texture of the greatest examples of English verse'

'[it] fits snugly into the tradition of the verse epistle out of which the dramatic monologue developed.'

[he] explores humanity's most profound experience: not just madness, but also terror, melancholy and (not least) laughter … In this view [he] is neither the 'authentic voice of disaffected working class youth', nor a 'nasty little yob', but a rapper whose genius is, principally, poetic.'

Foden was writing, not about some famous poet but about the lyrics of Eminem, the controversial rapper. The song he describes is 'Stan', Eminem's address to an obsessed fan, which ends with Stan drowning his girlfriend in the boot of his car. Foden compares what Eminem is doing here with Robert Browning, the nineteenth century poet, who wrote monologues in the voices of characters, some of whom were cold and calculating murderers.

■ Read these extracts from letters to the newspaper, responding to Giles Foden's article.

'Giles Foden may be right or wrong on Eminem being a modern day Robert Browning. However I'll wager his lyrics will generate far more intelligent discussion over the coming years than those of the so-called Popstars who have plagued our television screens over the past weeks.'

'I assume *The Guardian* will be advertising for a new deputy literary editor once the men in white coats have taken poor Giles Foden into secure accommodation. Comparing the ravings of Eminem with those of poets like Browning and Eliot is preposterous.'

'Poetic or not, Eminem's lyrics legitimise the growth in violence against women and gays. In failing to call Eminem to account, Foden's piece is not criticism at all; merely parasitic gush.'

'I sincerely hope that Giles Foden is practising the irony that he praises Eminem so lavishly for … Eminem and everything he stands for, ironic or not, is offensive. Full stop. Which doesn't in itself make it bad art, but it does preclude pretentious articles from otherwise respected writers and broadsheets. Please don't do it again.'

'The interesting question is not how good Eminem is, but why it is that such angry and violent lyrics speak so loudly to people. Eminem's songs are, among other things, intense cries of pain; it is a world in pain that has so taken him to its heart.'

Airing your views   Class work

■   Have a short discussion, in which you discuss some of your views.

■   Use the ideas raised in the debate to write an email letter to *The Guardian* with your view on whether Eminem should be hailed as a great poet, praised as a brilliant rapper or banned from recording and performing such offensive songs.

Powerful lyrics

Individual research   Homework

■   Think of one example of your own of a song that seems to you to have powerful, interesting lyrics. Choose something that is usable in the classroom!

■   Find a way of getting hold of the words. You could get them from a CD cover, from sheet music, from an Internet lyrics site, or by transcribing the subtitles on *Top of the Pops* or other music programmes on TV (You can get them to come up on screen by going to CEEFAX 888).

■   Write a paragraph explaining what you think is special about these song lyrics. Why are they particularly interesting or enjoyable for you? Is it because:
 - they are about an interesting or unusual subject
 - they tell a story
 - you keep finding more in them as you listen, rather than getting bored with them
 - they are relevant to you and your life
 - they use rhyme cleverly
 - they capture an emotion well
 - they have interesting images (metaphors, similes and symbols)
 - they use aspects of sound particularly well (rhythm, alliteration and so on).

Reading and writing lyrics

Sharing your lyrics Group work
- Present the lyrics that you chose to your group. You could play the song, read the lyrics to them and read aloud what you wrote about the lyrics. At the end of each presentation, pause to allow other people in the class to agree, disagree or add their own comments.

Writing your own lyrics

- Now that you have thought about how song lyrics work and what kind of lyrics you like, you are going to try writing some words of your own.

- Try writing the first verse of a song in three or four different styles. For instance:
  - as rap
  - as a romantic ballad for a boy band
  - as dance music
  - as a pop song
  - as hip hop
  - as a song for a solo singer/songwriter.

- Choose one to work up into a finished song. Remember to think about it as a song rather than a poem – will it have a chorus, repeated refrains, or repeated verses, to give it a musical structure?

Words and music
- If you play an instrument, or enjoy singing, try putting your words to music, as a complete song. (You could experiment with writing the words and the music together, or composing the music first, then putting the words to the music, to see which works best.)

Travis, from the video of 'Driftwood'

A poetry reading trail

In this unit you will:
- read a translation of an extract from a famous story, told as a poem
- explore the way painters and writers throughout history have interpreted and used this story
- compare different interpretations of the same story
- learn how to write a critical essay
- write your own version of a myth.

What sort of story is this?

Investigating a story   Class work
- Read the notes in the box below and talk about whether it reminds you of any stories you've heard or read in books, films or newspapers.

A boy and his father – a clash between the generations – the father tries to tell him what to do – the boy promises to follow his father's advice but he's having such a great time – he forgets his father's warnings – he takes risks, stupid ones – he ends up in big trouble – he dies a violent death – his father is heartbroken – why didn't he listen?

What kind of story is it? Pair work
- Talk about what sort of story this might be the outline for. Use the ideas suggested here to start you thinking. Could it be any – or all – of these?

A tabloid front page story	A children's drama on ITV	A Greek myth
A children's novel	The storyline for a musical	A storyline in a soap opera

- Talk about the thinking behind your choices. For example, you might suggest it could be a soap opera because the storylines of many soap operas feature family conflict and tragedy.

The themes of the story   Pair and whole class work
- Read the outline of the story again and make a note of any themes you think it might raise. For instance, do you think it raises any of the themes listed on the next page?

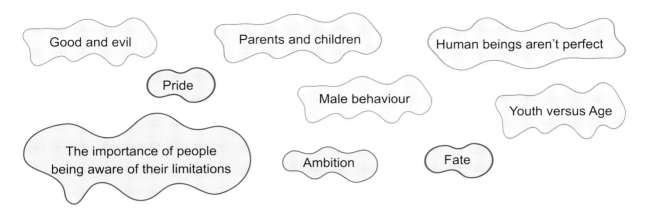

- Take it in turns to feed back your ideas about the story outline.

Dictionary work   Homework
- Find out and record the meanings of the following words:

Exile   Pining   Peril   Awe   Fatal

Reading a Greek myth – the story of Daedalus and Icarus

The original version   Class work

The story outline you have been working on is based on the legend of Daedalus and his son Icarus, one of the Greek myths. It has been re-told many times since it was first written down, as a poem, by the writer Ovid. Ovid lived from 43BC till 17AD.

- You are going to listen to the story, but first feed back your research on some of the words that appear in it (exile, pining, peril, awe and fatal). Talk about any similarities or connections you notice in the meanings of the words.

- Now listen to Ovid's poem being read aloud and share your first thoughts about it.

Exploring patterns   Pair work

- Look at the poem to see if you can see any of the patterns and contrasts suggested here.

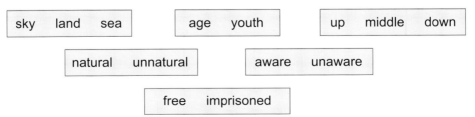

- Then, on a large sheet of paper, create a series of spider diagrams or webs, to show your ideas about the patterns in the poem. Take short quotations from the poem and note them on your diagrams. Explain how you think the pattern works.

Daedalus and Icarus

Hating the isle of *Crete and the long years
Of exile, Daedalus was pining for
His native land, but seas on every side
Imprisoned him. 'Though land and sea,' he thought,
'The king may bar to me, at least the sky
Is open; through the sky I'll set my course.
Minos may own all else; he does not own
The air.' So then to unimagined arts
He set his mind and altered nature's laws.

   Row upon row of feathers he arranged,
The smallest first, then larger ones, to form
A growing graded shape, as rustic pipes
Rise in a gradual slope of lengthening reeds;
Then bound the middle and the base with wax
And flaxen threads, and bent them, so arranged,
Into a gentle curve to imitate
Wings of a real bird. His boy stood by,
Young Icarus, who, blithely unaware
He plays with his own peril, tries to catch
Feathers that float upon the wandering breeze,
Or softens with his thumb the yellow wax,
And by his laughing mischief interrupts
His father's wondrous work. Then, when the last
Sure touch was given, the craftsman poised himself
On his twin wings and hovered in the air.

   Next he prepared his son. 'Take care', he said,
'To fly a middle course, lest if you sink
Too low the waves may weight your feathers; if
Too high, the heat may burn them. Fly half-way
Between the two. And do not watch the stars,
The Great Bear or the Wagoner or Orion,
With his drawn sword, to steer by. Set your course
Where I shall lead.' He fixed the strange new wings
On his son's shoulders and instructed him
How he should fly; and, as he worked and warned,

The old man's cheeks were wet, the father's hands
Trembled. He kissed his son (the last kisses
He'd ever give) and rising on his wings
He flew ahead, anxious for his son's sake,
Just like a bird that from its lofty nest
Launches a tender fledgling in the air.
Calling his son to follow, schooling him
In that fatal apprenticeship, he flapped
His wings and watched the boy flapping behind.

   An angler fishing with his quivering rod,
A lonely shepherd propped upon his crook,
A ploughman leaning on his plough, looked up
And gazed in awe, and thought they must be gods
That they could fly. **Delos and Paros lay
Behind them now; Samos, great Juno's isle,
Was on the left, Lebinthos on the right
And honey-rich Calymne, when the boy
Began to enjoy his thrilling flight and left
His guide to roam the ranges of the heavens,
And soared too high. The scorching sun so close
Softened the fragrant wax that bound his wings;
The wax melted; his waving arms were bare;
Unfledged, they had no purchase on the air!
And calling to his father as he fell,
The boy was swallowed in the blue sea's swell,
The blue sea that for ever bears his name.
His wretched father, now no father, cried
'Oh, Icarus, where are you? Icarus,
Where shall I look, where find you?' On the waves
He saw the feathers. Then he cursed his skill,
And buried his boy's body in a grave,
And still that island keeps the name he gave.

Ovid (from *Metamorphosis*)

*Crete is a large island off the coast of Greece, ruled in those times by Minos.

**Delos, Paros, Samos, Lebinthos and Calymne are all smaller islands. Juno was a Goddess, wife of Jupiter.

Presenting the patterns Class work

■ Take it in turns to present your ideas about *one* of the patterns to the rest of the class. Share your responses to the patterns different pairs have noticed.

■ Talk about what the patterns reveal about what's important in this telling.

■ Look back at the themes on page 75. Which do you find most interesting and important in *this* telling of the story?

■ Which of these themes do you think would be most interesting or important for the readers suggested below?

  - A 20th century teenage boy
  - A 20th century woman
  - Someone with a strong religious faith
  - A young child
  - A parent
  - A scientist or astronomer in Ancient Greece
  - A painter looking for a subject for a painting

A short written response Homework

■ Write a paragraph, as a short response to this story, in the voice of one of these readers. Draw attention to the themes you think this reader would find most important, for instance, 'As a parent, when I read this story I felt really...'

Re-telling the story of Daedalus and Icarus

Comparing interpretations Class work

■ Listen to a few of the paragraphs in the voices of different readers. Talk about the probable similarities and differences between the responses of these readers.

The story of Icarus in art Individual and pair work

■ Imagine that you have been asked to do a painting to illustrate Ovid's story of Icarus. What would your painting show? Either jot down ideas about it or draw a quick sketch of it, annotating the sketch with ideas for shapes, colours and style.

■ Describe your ideas to a partner, using your notes or sketch to help you. Talk about any similarities and differences in the way you have represented the story.

■ Share your ideas for the ways the story could be represented in a painting. Which themes have different readers emphasised? Which aspects have they ignored?

Painting the story of Icarus

■ Look at the paintings on page 78 and 79. They both represent the story of Icarus.

■ Write down exactly what you see.

The Fall of Icarus, 1981 (oil on canvas) by André Durand (contemporary artist).
Private collection/Bridgeman Art Library.

Landscape with the Fall of Icarus, c.1558-66 (oil on canvas) by Peter the Elder Brueghel (c.1515-69). Musées Royaux des Beaux-Arts de Belgique. Brussels, Belgium, Bridgeman Art Library.

Sharing your ideas   Group work

■   Join up with two or three other people. Read out to each other your descriptions of what you saw in the paintings. Talk about any differences in what you noticed.

■   Now talk about any similarities and differences in the painters' interpretations of the story of Daedalus and Icarus, using the prompts below.

- What have each of the painters chosen to emphasise?
- What aspects of Ovid's story have they included or left out?
- Look back at the list of possible themes for the story. Think about which ones are emphasised by each of the paintings and add any others.
- Which do you prefer and why? (You might want to think about: what caught your eye; the use of colour, shapes and other visual qualities; the ideas suggested; what you find appealing or intriguing or interesting about it.)

Writing about the paintings   Homework

Write a short analytical piece of writing on one of the paintings. You should include a paragraph on each of the following:
- a description of the painting
- an explanation of the way the painter has used and interpreted the story (with qoutations from Ovid's poem to show the connections between the two)
- your personal response to the painting and how it relates to the poem.

Written versions of the Icarus story

Over the centuries many writers as well as painters have made use of the Icarus legend, re-telling it for their own purposes. What they have done with the original story will have been influenced by:
- their own individual character, tastes and interests
- the attitudes, beliefs and concerns of their society
- the ways in which language has changed over time
- the ways in which literature has changed over time.

Exploring the story of Icarus through time   Pair and class work

The short quotations on page 81 are from poems from different centuries. They all make use of the Icarus story.

■   In pairs read the quotations and try to match the century to the quotation. In each case suggest one or two reasons for your decision.

Late 14th century
End of 16th century
End of 20th century

Reading through time

■ Spend a few minutes talking about what helped you identify the century each extract belongs to. For instance, was it the ideas, attitudes and beliefs expressed, the language or the form and style in which it was written? You might find it helpful to make a few notes of your ideas, in a grid like the one shown here. The first one has been started, to show the kinds of points you might make.

■ Share your ideas as a whole class.

Extract	Period	Ideas, attitudes & beliefs	Language	Literary Form and style

1

  'Seest thou any toun
Or ought thou knowest yonder doun?'
I sayde, 'Nay.' 'No wonder nys,'
Quod he, 'for half so high as this
Nas Alixandre Macedo;
Ne the kyng, Daun Scipio,
That saw in drem, at poynt devys,
Helle and erthe and paradys;
Ne eke the wrechche Dedalus,
Ne his child, nyce Ykarus,
That fleigh so highe that the hete
Hys wynges malt, and he fel wete …

2

Daddy, Daddy is that you?
Listen I don't have much time OK.
But I wanted to say, right
It's back to the drawing board Daddy
The whole contraption is a no no.

3

Love wing'd my Hopes and taught me how to fly
   Far from base earth, but not to mount too high:
     For true pleasure
     Lives in measure,
      Which if men forsake,
Blinded they into folly run and grief for pleasure take.

A closer reading of the poems   Pair work

■ Read and explore *one* of the poems on pages 83 – 86 in more detail. Ask yourself the questions on the next page.

- What aspects of the original story does it focus on?
- What does it do with the original story? Does it update it, or make it funny? Does it tell it unemotionally, or make it dramatic and tragic? Does it use the story to put across a message or moral, use it to say something about modern life, or use it as a metaphor in a completely different story?
- What do you find enjoyable about it? Is it the sound of the words, the rhythm or rhyme? Is it the tone, the creation of a mood, a visual picture or a situation? Is it the telling of the story or the way language is used?
- What kind of reader do you think it would appeal to? (Look at the list on page 76 to remind you of your thoughts about different readers' possible responses to Ovid's telling of the story.)

Writing about the poem   Homework
- Write a short piece about the poem, exploring:
  - how it uses the Icarus story
  - how it works as a poem
  - your personal response to it.

Writing your own version of the Icarus story

Icarus for the 21st century   Class work
- Brainstorm all the ways you think the story of Icarus could be re-told for a reader in the 21st century. Use the ideas suggested here to start you thinking:
  - as a warning about reckless behaviour
  - as a moan about male behaviour
  - as a political song about refugees from a brutal dictator.

A modern pop song   Individual work
- Write your version of the Icarus myth, as a modern pop song. You will need to make the following decisions:
  - what slant you want to give the song
  - the themes you want to draw out
  - the point of view from which you will tell the story
  - the tone (for example, humorous, serious, angry)
  - the type of song (for example, ballad, rap, folk, American and so on)
  - the structure and style of the song (for example, the number of verses; whether there will be a chorus; whether it will rhyme).

Getting feed back   Pair work
- Read the first draft of your song to your partner and make a note of their response.

- Make any alterations you think will improve the song.

Performing your songs   Class work

■   Take it in turns to perform your songs to each other.

■   As you listen to the songs, make a note of the themes each person has chosen to emphasise and the slant they have taken.

■   Share your responses to the Icarus songs.

Icarus by Mobile

Daddy, Daddy is that you?
Listen I don't have much time OK.
But I wanted to say, right
It's back to the drawing board Daddy
The whole contraption is a no no.
The wings?
No, the wings worked fine
Couldn't fault the wings in any way
The wings were ace
And your calculations on the stresses
Re wind and feathers
Spot on!
Likewise the pinion tolerances
And remember that flap factor
That gave us both such sleepless nights
Let me tell you
Those flaps worked like a dream.
But Daddy
Oh Daddy
How could you forget the sun!
I don't have much time
So listen OK.
We're talking equations here
Just let me spell it out for you:
Solar heat + bees wax + ambition =
Total Meltdown and I mean total
Which equals, to put it simply,
Your boy Icarus on collision course
With something called the Earth.
Daddy I don't have much time
Let me give you my co-ordinates

For the pick up
OK stretch of headland and a bay
Visibility good, outlook calm
And hey
Am I lucky
Or am I lucky!
There's a galleon anchored near the shore
Looks like Icarus
Is in for an early pick up this fine morning.
And over there some poor old farmer's
Ploughing through a field of stones
And here's an old boy with a fishing pole and
Listen Daddy
Would you believe
Some guy just out of frame
Is painting the whole thing.
And now I'm waving Daddy, waving
Any minute now they'll all look up and
So listen Daddy I don't have much time
I'm going to start screaming soon OK.
Can you still hear me?
I don't have much
Daddy, I just wanted to ask
You know
About my mum
Was she
Listen Daddy
I don't have much time
I

Gareth Owen

Icarus

Love wing'd my Hopes and taught me how to fly
Far from base earth, but not to mount too high:
    For true pleasure
    Lives in measure,
    Which if men forsake,
Blinded they into folly run and grief for pleasure take.

But my vain Hopes, proud of their new-taught flight,
Enamour'd sought to woo the sun's fair light,
    Whose rich brightness
    Moved their lightness
    To aspire so high
That all scorch'd and consumed with fire now drown'd in
                woe they lie.

And none but Love their woeful hap did rue,
For Love did know that their desires were true;
    Though fate frownèd
    And now drownèd
    They in sorrow dwell,
It was the purest light of heav'n for whose fair love they fell.

**Anonymous,
1601**

Icarus Shmicarus

If you never spend your money
you know you'll always have some cash.
If you stay cool and never burn
you'll never turn to ash.
If you lick the boots that kick you
then you'll never feel the lash,
and if you crawl along the ground
at least you'll never crash.
So why why why –
WHAT MADE YOU THINK YOU COULD FLY?

Adrian Mitchell

Mrs. Icarus

I'm not the first or the last
to stand on a hillock,
watching the man she married
prove to the world
he's a total, utter, absolute, Grade A pillock.

Carol Ann Duffy

From **The House of Fame**

'By thy trouthe, yond adoun,
Wher that thou knowest any toun,
Or hous, or any other thing.
And whan thou hast of ought knowyng,
Looke that thou warne me,
And y anoon shal telle the
How fer that thou art now therfro.'
  And y adoun gan loken thoo,
And beheld feldes and playnes,
And now hilles, and now mountaynes,
Now valeyes, now forestes,
And now unnethes grete bestes;
Now ryveres, now citees,
Now tounes, and now grete trees,
Now shippes seyllynge in the see.
  But thus sone in a while he
Was flowen fro the ground so hye
That al the world, as to myn yë,
No more semed than a prikke;

Or elles was the air so thikke
That y ne myghte not discerne.
With that he spak to me as yerne,
And seyde, 'Seest thou any toun
Or ought thou knowest yonder doun?'
I sayde, 'Nay.' 'No wonder nys,'
Quod he, 'for half so high as this
Nas Alixandre Macedo;
Ne the kyng, Daun Scipio,
That saw in drem, at poynt devys,
Helle and erthe and paradys;
Ne eke the wrechche Dedalus,
Ne his child, nyce Ykarus,
That fleigh so highe that the hete
Hys wynges malt, and he fel wete
In myd the see, and ther he dreynte,
For whom was maked moch compleynte.

Chaucer

To a Friend Whose Work Has Come to Triumph

Consider Icarus, pasting those sticky wings on,
testing that strange little tug at his shoulder blade,
and think of that first flawless moment over the lawn
of the labyrinth. Think of the difference it made!
There below are the trees, as awkward as camels;
and here are the shocked starlings pumping past
and think of innocent Icarus who is doing quite well:
larger than a sail, over the fog and the blast
of the plushy ocean he goes. Admire his wings!
Feel the fire at his neck and see how casually
he glances up and is caught, wondrously tunneling
into that hot eye. Who cares that he fell back to the
sea?
See him acclaiming the sun and come plunging down
while his sensible daddy goes straight into town.

Anne Sexton

From **Henry VI Part 3**

Henry talking about his son

Henry:
The bird that hath been limed in a bush,
With trembling wings misdoubteth every bush;
And I the hapless male to one sweet bird,
Have now the fatal object in my eye
Where my poor young was lim'd. was caught, and killed.
Glo:
Why, what a peevish fool was that of Crete
That taught his son the office of a fowl!
And yet, for all his wings, the fool was drown'd.

Henry:
I, Daedalus; my poor boy, Icarus;
Thy father, Minos, that denied our course;
The sun that sear'd the wings of my sweet boy,
Thy brother Edward; and thyself, the sea
Whose envious gulf did swallow up his life.
All, kill me with thy weapon, not with words!
My breast can better brook thy dagger's point
Than can my ears that tragic history.
But wherefore dost thou come? Is't for my life?

William Shakespeare

John Hegley

In this unit you will:
- listen to John Hegley perform and talk about a selection of his poems
- explore the use of rhythm and rhyme
- consider the way humour works in poetry
- write and perform a poem of your own.

Introducing John Hegley

Watching the video Class viewing

■ Watch the poet, John Hegley, perform and talk about a selection of his poems. The titles of the poems are listed here.

Super sunburn
Vision
Poem about my glasses
I feel like a suitcase
Love poem by my dog
Rowena
Poem de terre
A Declaration of Need

Sharing first responses Pair and class work

■ Talk about first responses to the performance. Pick out one thing that you found particularly striking or memorable. This could be because it was funny, or strange, or annoying or thought-provoking. In your own words, try and explain the reason for your reaction.

■ Take it in turns to read out your memorable moments. How many of these are about the performance? How many are about the poems? Or are they about a combination of the two?

Other readers respond Individual work

Printed on the next page are some of the comments one Year 9 class made after watching this performance.

■ Read through the comments and talk about whether or not you agree with them.

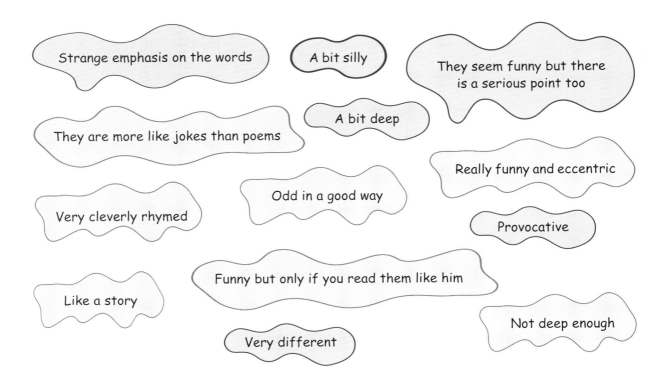

Strange emphasis on the words

A bit silly

They seem funny but there is a serious point too

A bit deep

They are more like jokes than poems

Really funny and eccentric

Odd in a good way

Very cleverly rhymed

Provocative

Funny but only if you read them like him

Like a story

Not deep enough

Very different

■ Choose one comment you agree with and one comment you disagree with. Use these as the starting point for writing a paragraph on your own first response to John Hegley's poetry.

A poetry performance

Listening to 'Rowena'   Class viewing and pair work
The poem 'Rowena' is printed here without line breaks.

■ Listen again to John Hegley's performance of 'Rowena' and mark a photocopy of the poem to show how you think it should be set out.

I was keener on Rowena than I'd ever been on anyone before and one night she came round she said she wanted some excitement then she pulled me to the ground I took off my glasses turned the telly down and started getting down to business after I'd done the business I felt fantastic like I'd melted in a flame but Rowena never felt the same she said she had more excitement when her last gas bill came then she kicked my glasses across the room damaged one of the little windows and twisted the frame up oh Rowena oh woe woe Rowena she said I was dead below the belt and above the belt and as I felt around for my glasses you don't know how I felt (around for my glasses) she said I had done the business like I was the only one there she said I was totally unaware of what she wanted and that all I wanted was someone who just wanted to lie there I said look what you've done to my glasses they are in need of repair but did Rowena care about my distress the answer is not yes she said those glasses suit you now John they are a mess she said you get up my nose and it's time I had a pick she said she'd had more fun in bed with a dead matchstick I said when were you in bed with a dead matchstick Rowena? jealousy's a terrible thing and she said hold your breath for ever that should do the trick you're even thicker than your glasses less of that Rowena I commanded don't you ever talk about my glasses like that again alright I said but she'd already gone I never saw her go though I never had my glasses on

■   Compare your ideas and talk about how you made your decisions. Some of the clues you can get from the performance are suggested here:
    – the words he chooses to emphasise
    – rhythm
    – rhyme
    – pauses
    – body language
    – facial expression
    – what he does with the pitch of his voice
    – timing
    – repetition.

■   Listen to the poem again and mark your photocopy to show how it is performed.

Whole class discussion   Class work
■   Take it in turns to feed back your ideas about the lay out and performance of 'Rowena'.

Poems on the page
■   Now look at the poem as it was originally printed, on pages 95-96. Compare the printed version with the one you marked up after hearing it performed. Does anything surprise you? If so, talk about the reasons John Hegley might have written the poem in this way.

Exploring Hegley's humour

Which poems make you laugh?   Class work
■   Tell each other about the poems you find funny and why this is. (They are printed on pages 94–97.)

This is what John Hegley says he finds funny:
    – nice observations about life
    – humour that is committed, that makes a serious point
    – caricatures (caricatures are exaggerated, grotesque depictions of people)
    – exaggeration.

■   Find examples of each of these sorts of humour in the poems other than 'Rowena' and talk about how the humour works.

Humour in Rowena   Class work

■   Talk about the way the humour works in 'Rowena'. See if you can find examples of the different techniques John Hegley uses to make the poem funny. Record your discoveries in a table like the one shown here.

Technique	Example	Comment
Subject matter Setting up expectations and undermining them A gap between the subject and the way it is described (for example, talking about something ordinary as though it is very important) Double meanings and puns (including sexual innuendo) Exaggeration Rhyme Repetition Rhythm Representation on the page (for example, line breaks, different fonts, illustrations).		

Poems with a serious point?

Many of John Hegley's poems are funny, making the reader laugh (perhaps by saying the opposite of what is expected, by making an unusual or bizarre comparison or by writing about a subject not normally found in poetry). However, some of the poems also make a serious point. As Hegley says:

> Sometimes you have a point to make – a serious point. 'Vision' makes the point that it's quite good not to be overly worried about the colour of people's skins. But I think it is quite good not to make it seem as though you are taking yourself too seriously about these things. If you want to get your message across, it's always better to get it across with a joke if you can make one.
>
> Sometimes it's nice to be daft and serious together, like I am in 'A Declaration of Need'. This one I suppose is fairly daft all the way through and then at the end is a little bit more serious. I suppose I quite like mixing seriousness and daftness together.

The following quotations are taken from John Hegley's poems.

> the bright right handprints
> that my Dad would add to my arms and legs
> when I was bad

where nobody cares about the colour of your skin

| and they wonder why I break and they stick labels on me | | I'm not a normal person whatever that may be |

| I need you like a candle needs a moth if it's going to burn its wings off. | | He was hurt and he called me a dirty so-and-so. |

■   Talk about the points Hegley seems to be making in each of these quotations.

Are they poems to be read?

Some people argue that poems like John Hegley's only work when they are performed, not when they are read in a book.

■   What do you think? Now you have looked more closely at the way the poems are written you are in a good position to comment. Talk about how well the poems work on the page. What is added by hearing the funny poems performed by the poet? What about the more serious ones? Collect together all the different ideas and arguments. Choose quotations from the poems to support what you are saying.

Summing up your ideas   Class work

■   Pool all of your ideas about John Hegley's poetry, as a list of bullet points summing up what's interesting and special about him. Here is one to start you off:

John Hegley's poems work especially well as performances.

An introduction to John Hegley   Homework

■   Write an introduction to John Hegley for another year 9 class who have not read any of his poetry before, or seen him perform. Use the bullet points you have assembled in class to remind you of key ideas to write about. Add in examples and quotations to back up each point you make and analyse each quotation to explain your ideas more fully.

Writing poetry

John Hegley's writing process   Individual work

Printed below are some of the key things John Hegley says about the process of writing a poem.

■   Read through the comments and pull out the one thing you find most interesting about the way he writes.

> 'Poem de terre' is a way of writing about not being what somebody wants you to be. Rather than saying, 'Me and my dad argued,' it's moving it away one step. It's quite good to take another object and use it as a way of describing your feelings, how you are, how you want to be. On the other hand, 'Super sunburn' is about my dad and this is really just a straightforward telling rather than using something as a poetic device, an image like a potato. This is just me being me. It's a fairly straightforward poem.

> If you want to get your message across, it's always better to get it across with a joke if you can make one. What happened when I started performing was people used to shout out things about my glasses and I've taken that on board and used it in my favour. It's a little joke. It's a good way of dealing with things. It disarms people if you say something first.

> Sometimes I get an inspiration to write something and the stuff comes quite easily. Something happens and you've got something you want to write about. Sometimes you have to work at something like the 'I need you' poem – 'A Declaration of Need'. It was quite a laborious process but I enjoyed writing it. It wasn't just one idea or one image. It's lots of ideas.

> My poems sometimes are jokes and sometimes they are lists and sometimes they are stories. But there is always a certain density in the language. And I do like rhythm. I do like rhyme. I try to bring those things in. To some extent they wouldn't be poems without those things. They would be stories or jokes or lists.

Writing a poem   Individual work

John Hegley goes on to suggest some of the things you could do with his ideas about writing poetry.

■   Choose the idea which appeals to you most and use it as a way into writing your own poem to perform.

 - Subjects which are important to you (for example, your ambition, a treasured possession or memory)
 - Things which you know about and are an expert on (for example, football, music, PlayStation)

- Things other people *think* they don't want to hear about (your everyday routine, your favourite pair of jeans)
- Topics which are not normally the subject of poetry (for example, brushing your teeth, HB pencils, bus stops, fridge magnets)
- An ordinary subject from a peculiar point of view (getting ready to go on holiday from the point of view of your cat)
- Describing what you want to be
- Describing the difference between what you are like and what other people *think* you are like

Getting feedback   Pair and group work

■   Take turns to comment on each other's poems. You will need to listen to the poems as well as read them. Focus on any words or lines which prove tricky. Make changes to your poems, in the light of your partner's comments.

■   Get together with another pair to listen to each others' poems. Listen to each others' comments and note down any suggestions for changes.

Writing a final version   Homework

■   Write up a final version of the poem.

■   Write a paragraph or two explaining the choices you made and the way in which the poem changed in response to other people's feedback.

Performing your poem

Planning the performance   Individual work
You are going to prepare your own poem for performance.

■   Remind yourself of all the different techniques John Hegley uses during the performance, to bring his poetry to life. A few ideas are suggested here to start you thinking:
    - hand gestures
    - looking at the audience
    - long pauses to keep the listener waiting
    - using interesting or unusual facial gestures.

■   Draw up a set of criteria for judging a successful performance poem.

■   Annotate a copy of your poem to show how you will perform it. If you have chosen to write in the style of John Hegley, you could imitate his style of performance too. If you have written in a style of your own, you could create a persona for yourself. This does not need to be anything like your real self.

Practising the performance Pair work

■ Work in pairs or small groups to practise your performance. Remember to use what you have learned from John Hegley to help you make your performance effective.

A class performance Class work

■ Take it in turns to perform your poem. You could do this in small groups or as a whole class.

Super sunburn

super sunburn
is what my brother
called the bright right handprints
that my Dad would add to my arms and legs
when I was bad
he thought up the title
one night while he was eating my supper
regular burns were handed out
for shouting at my sister
when she failed to collect the rent
after I had landed on one of her properties in
       Monopoly
but the biggest attack
was for when my Dad said he was fed up
to the back teeth with me
and I pointed out that he never had any back teeth
my brother said that the marks I received on this
       occasion
were excellent

Vision

I have a notion of a nation
where greener grass is
where everyone is trying on everybody else's glasses
where nobody cares about the colour of your skin
or the colour of the case that your glasses are kept in

Poem about my glasses

I look after my spectacles
because they look after me
without my spectacles
where would I be
I'd probably be standing here
but I'd have a job to see
properly

I feel like a suitcase

they fill me up with just about
as much as I can take
then they put some more in
and they wonder why I break
and they stick labels on me

Love poem by my dog

I saw you in the park
I wanted to be your friend
I tunnelled my snout
up your non-barking end

Rowena

I was keener on Rowena
than I'd ever been on anyone before
and one night she came round
she said she wanted some excitement
then she pulled me to the ground
I took off my glasses
turned the telly down
and started getting down to business
after I'd done the business
I felt FANTASTIC
like I'd melted in a flame
but Rowena never felt the same
she said she had more excitement
when her last gas bill came
then she kicked my glasses across the room
damaged one of the little windows
and twisted the frame
up
oh Rowena oh woe woe Rowena
she said I was dead below the belt
and above the belt
and as I felt around for my glasses
you don't know how I felt
(around for my glasses)
she said I had done the business
like I was the only one there
she said I was totally unaware
of what she wanted and that all I wanted
was someone who just wanted to lie there

I said look what you've done to my glasses
they are in need of repair
but did Rowena care about my distress
the answer is not yes
she said those glasses suit you now
John
they are a mess
she said you get up my nose
and it's time I had a pick
she said she'd had more fun in bed
with a dead matchstick
I said when were you in bed
with a dead matchstick Rowena?
jealousy's a terrible thing
and she said hold your breath for ever
that should do the trick
you're even thicker than your glasses
less of that Rowena I commanded
don't you ever talk about my glasses like that again
ALRIGHT I said
but she'd already gone
I never saw her go though [1]

[1] I never had my glasses on

Poem de terre

I'm not a normal person
whatever that may be
there is something very very vegetable
about me,
this human skin I'm skulking in
it's only there for show,
I'm a potato.
When I told my father
it was something of a blow,
he was hurt
and he called me a dirty so-and-so.
He kicked up a racket
and he grabbed me by the jacket;
I said, 'Daddy will you pack it in
I need you for my father not my foe
Daddy, will you try and help me grow,
won't you love me for my blemishes

Humorous poems

and look me in the eye
before one of us is underground
and the other says goodbye?'
And he said, 'No.'

When I was a schoolboy
I never knew why
I was so crap at cross-country running
but now I know
why I was so slow.
I'm a potato.

A Declaration of Need

I need you like a novel needs a plot.
I need you like the greedy need a lot.
I need you like a hovel needs a certain level of grottiness
to qualify.
I need you like acne cream needs spottiness.
Like a calendar needs a week.
Like a colander needs a leek.
Like people need to seek out what life on Mars is.
Like hospitals need vases.
I need you.
I need you like a zoo needs a giraffe.
I need you like a psycho needs a path.
I need you like King Arthur needed a table
that was more than just a table for one.
I need you like a kiwi needs a fruit.
I need you like a wee wee needs a route out of the body.
I need you like Noddy needed little ears,
just for the contrast.
I need you like bone needs marrow.
I need you like straight needs narrow.
I need you like the broadest bean needs something else on
  the plate
before it can participate
in what you might describe as a decent meal.
I need you like a cappuccino needs froth.
I need you like a candle needs a moth
if it's going to burn its wings off.

Lit Pops

Introducing *Lit Pops*

In 1998 Channel 4 showed a series called *Lit Pops*. Each night, at around 8.00p.m., the channel broadcast a single poem performed by the poet, with visual images and a sound track. You will be working on two poems from the series.

■ Before you start working on the unit, talk about the title *Lit Pops*. What does it make you expect? What kind of programmes do you think they will be? What view of poetry do you think they will put across?

Breadline

'Just a minute' on the subject of the breadline   Class work

One of the poems you are going to see performed is called 'Breadline'. The dictionary definition of breadline says:
- breadline – a queue of people waiting for free food given out by a government agency or charity organisation
- on the breadline - impoverished; living at subsistence level.

■ Play 'Just a Minute' to get you thinking about this subject. One of you has to talk for one minute without hesitation or repetition on the subject of 'the breadline'. Anyone else in the class can challenge you if they believe you have hesitated or repeated yourself (small words don't count). The challenger then has to continue for the time remaining. The teacher is the referee.

Why 'water' and why 'wine'?   Group work

'Water' and 'wine' are two words repeated throughout the poem 'Breadline'.

■ Talk about any familiar phrases, sayings or events associated with these words. What expectations do these associations set up for you about the poem?

Rhythm and rhyme   Pair work

Performance poetry is often not available in published form. The poem you are going to watch and hear has been transcribed so that you can see what it looks like on the page.

■ Work on a photocopy of the text. The first section of the poem is printed below, but not arranged into lines. See whether you can arrange it into lines by attending to:
  – rhythm
  – rhyme
  – repetition
  – alliteration
  – anything else that you notice.
Mark with the symbol // the points where you think there should be a line break.

■ When you have worked out a version you're happy with, practise saying it aloud. Make a group with another pair and listen to one another's versions.

■ What was easy or difficult about this activity? How much agreement was there about the way the poem should be marked?

> Couldn't afford no water never no couldn't afford no wine couldn't afford no nothing when you back up on the breadline couldn't afford no water couldn't afford no wine couldn't afford nothing you got yours oh where's mine I was afraid I was gonna get laid off they made off with his pension why he wasn't paid off not a penny the company tell him not to worry too old to get hold of another job in a hurry so don't blame economy we'd rather have apology my pride overrides that kind of type of poverty recessionary reinforcably why welcome back my friend Jack welcome back into the bread line couldn't afford no water couldn't afford no wine couldn't afford nothing when you're back up on the breadline

Rhythm   Group work

  'It don't mean a thing if it ain't got that swing' (Duke Ellington).

Duke Ellington was talking about music, but could this description also apply to other things, like ordinary speech, poetry and other kinds of writing?

■ Think of three or four examples of spoken or written texts where the rhythm is important. For instance, one might be nursery rhymes, where the words themselves don't always mean a lot but children enjoy the bouncy rhythms. 'Pat-a-cake, pat-a-cake baker's man' or 'Hickory dickory dock' are two examples of this.

Roget's Thesaurus offers the following associated words to go with the word 'rhythm':

Accent	Beat	Cadence	Flow	Time
Lilt	Measure	Metre	Movement	
Pattern	Pulse	Swing	Tempo	

At first some of these words might seem to have little to do with rhythm. Some of them, for example, 'flow' and 'lilt' take a bit of thinking about.

■ Pick one of the words on the previous page and write a statement in which you explain its connection with rhythm. The example below shows you what to do.

'Flow': rhythm keeps the poem or song going. It allows the language and ideas to move smoothly and connect with each other, like a river.

Expectations about the poet – voice   Class work

■ From what you have read and discussed so far, make some predictions about the kind of person you think created and performed 'Breadline'. Think about gender, age, race, beliefs, tone of voice and so on. Back up your ideas with evidence from the text.

JC001

The poet's name is JCOO1.

■ Talk about how you expect this name to be spoken and why he might have chosen it for himself.

Watching 'Breadline'   Class viewing

■ Watch the performance of 'Breadline'

■ Now discuss your first reactions. How close was the performance to the groups' predictions about:
 – rhythm
 – voice
 – performer?

Poems as argument

JC001 has appeared in the *Guinness Book of Records* as the world's fastest rapper.

■ Look at this list of some of the main features of rap music:
 – words spoken (sometimes improvised) very fast and put to music
 – lots of repetition of sounds, words and lines
 – a strong rhythm or beat
 – a powerful, sometimes angry, message, often making a social or political comment
 – the language of the street, rather than formal or poetic language
 – usually associated with black, urban youth and street style.

■ What new insights does it give you to think of 'Breadline' as a piece of rap music, rather than as a poem?

'Breadline' is an angry poem.

■ Talk about what you think the poet is angry about.

■ Find examples where the poet's anger comes across in the language and in the performance.

The poet/performer uses some of the same rhetorical techniques that are found in political speeches and argument.

- See how many of the following techniques you can find in 'Breadline' and talk about the effect of these in putting across the message of the poem:
  - listing things in 3s
  - rhetorical questions
  - repetition.

Visual montage Class viewing and group work

The meaning of this text lies not only in the words but in the 'visual montage' created around it, i.e. all the images that are edited together to go with the words.

- Watch 'Breadline' again with a copy of the text in front of you. Share the text out among the different groups so that different sections are covered.

- In your group, note down what you see alongside what you hear.

Breadline

4 and 3 and 2 and 1 and

Couldn't afford no water never no couldn't afford no wine
    Couldn't afford no nothing when you back up on the breadline
    Couldn't afford no water
    Couldn't afford no wine
    Couldn't afford nothing you got yours oh where's mine

I was afraid I was gonna get laid off
    They made off with his pension why he wasn't paid off
    Not a penny
    The company tell him not to worry
    Too old to get hold of another job in a hurry

So don't blame economy
    We'd rather have apology
    My pride overides that kind of type of poverty
    Recessionary reinforcably why
    Welcome back my friend Jack welcome back into the breadline

Couldn't afford no water
    Couldn't afford no wine
    Couldn't afford nothing when you're back up on the breadline

---

Couldn't afford no water
Couldn't afford no wine
Couldn't afford nothing you got yours and where's mine.

Lady that I knows got baby that'll grow
A single parent depression that push you past peril
Got no maintenance indeed to bring in the feed
So now you got a million bucks to go out and breed

I keep forgetting got another good friend that
Got a job through agency that be driving me insane
No nanny no granny no pennies could ever find
The childminder's money when you're back upon the breadline

Couldn't afford no water
Couldn't afford no wine
Couldn't afford nothing when you're back up on the breadline

Couldn't afford no water
Couldn't afford no wine
Couldn't afford nothing you got yours and where's mine.

After the damages of 1980s avarice and 1990s decline
To the financial savages making mismanaged
The monetary mentality make you send out your sibling for a piffling salary

Who cares about the spirit?
Can't afford soul in the cardboard castle
Where the cashless brood
Where more and more they come for the
Smaller and smaller portions
It's a sort of a poor war

Poor sick and needy bleedin' me dry
'til you lookin at a mirror and you see its I and I
Don't deny the facts that you find in your mind

Welcome back Jack
Welcome back to the breadline

Couldn't afford no water
Couldn't afford no wine
Couldn't afford nothing when you're back up on the breadline

> Couldn't afford no water
> Couldn't afford no wine
> Couldn't afford nothing you got yours and where's mine.
>
> hit it
>
> Couldn't afford no water
> Couldn't afford no wine
> Couldn't afford nothing when you're back up on the breadline
>
> Couldn't afford no water
> Couldn't afford no wine
> Couldn't afford nothing you got yours and where's mine.
> On the bread line
>
> **JC001**

The images in the video

■ Discuss the range and choice of images.

■ Are they literal or abstract? Use these definitions to help you think about the difference between the two.

A literal image is one which is a straightforward picture of the object it is representing, such as the loaf of bread.

An abstract image is one which suggests an idea or feeling in a more metaphorical way, for instance using a dead rose to represent death.

■ Which works best, the literal or the abstract images?

■ What does the visual montage add to the words?

■ Discuss alternative image choices. Would the meaning stay the same?

Sound Class viewing

The video doesn't just put images with the original text. There are also music and sound effects.

■ Watch the video once more, this time focusing on the effect of the music and the poet's voice. How important are these elements to the overall effect of the poem? Do you think the poem works as well on the page as it does as a performance?

Ufo Woman

Before viewing Group work

You are going to look at one more *Lit Pop*. To help you think about its subject matter, spend a little time thinking about some of the words in the poem.

- Match the words below with their correct definitions.

Revelations	Ufo	UFO	Homo sapiens
Chameleon	Lagos	NF	Nefertiti
Dactylic and trochaic	Slave ship		

The chief port and commercial capital of Nigeria.

Two rhythms in poetry. One consists of three stresses, one long followed by two short (– - -). The other is two stresses, the first long and the second short (– -).

A lizard from Africa and Madagascar, with long slender legs, a prehensile tail and tongue, and the ability to change colour.

A ship used to transport slaves from Africa to the New World (America).

Unidentified Flying Object

A small political party of the right with racialist and other extremist policies.

The last book of the New Testament (bible) containing visionary descriptions of heaven, of conflicts between good and evil, and of the end of the world.

The specific name of modern man from Latin *homo* man + *sapiens* wise.

Word in one of the regional Nigerian languages pronounced oofoe; from the old days meaning weirdo, white, outsider, other.

14th century BC Egyptian queen

■ Compare your answers and talk about any ideas or expectations you now have about the poet and the poem.

The first verse

■ Read the first verse printed below and talk about what you think is going on in it.

- What do you notice about the use or absence of rhythm and rhyme?
- Who do you think is speaking in the poem?
- What do you notice about the language?

> Mother Earth. Heath Row. Terminal 5. Yo!
> Do I look hip in my space-hopper-green
> slingbacks, iridescent sky-blue-pink skin
> pants and hologram hair cut? Can I have
> my clothes back when you've finished with them, please?
> Hello! I just got offa the space ship.

Second verse

■ Now read the second verse and talk about it in the same way as you just did for the first. There may be observations you want to add such as:
- what you notice about the questioning pattern in the poem
- the different registers of English in the poem, such as street English, scientific language and so on
- the use and effect of colour in the poem.

> I've leant the language, read the VDU
> and watched the video twice. Mother Earth
> do *you* read *me*? Why then stamp my passport
> ALIEN at Heath Row? Did I come third
> in the World Race? Does my iridescent
> sky-blue-pink skin embarrass you, mother?

■ Try to summarise what you notice about the first two verses of this poem by completing the following statements.

One thing we think this poem is about is:
One question it leaves us asking is:

Feedback   Class work

■ As a whole class, listen to each others' statements carefully and discuss any points of uncertainty or disagreement.

■ Can you agree one or two statements which summarise what Patience Agbabi is saying in the first two verses of the poem?

Watch the video Pair viewing

■ After you have watched the video talk about your first reactions with a partner. Think back to your first ideas about the first two verses.

- How close were you to guessing the issues that the poet explores in the poem?
- What can you say about the style, appearance and character of the narrator in the video?
- What effect does the music and the poet's voice have on the poem itself? What is your response to these aspects of the video?

Read the text of the poem Group and class work

This is a long and complex poem. It appears in one of Patience Agbabi's published collections, *Transformatrix*.

■ Listen to her reading the poem on the video again, or take turns to read it aloud, this time following the words on the page.

■ Talk about how Agbabi has used aspects of the *written* language to develop her ideas and create interesting effects. Amongst other things you might like to look at the following:
- punctuation
- italics
- capital letters
- spelling
- line breaks.

■ Choose *one* of the aspects of the poem listed below. Focus on it for a report back to the whole class.

- The way the poet uses rhyme and other sound effects, like assonance and alliteration. (How much? Where in the line? What's the effect?)
- The way the poet uses repetition. (How much? Where? What's the effect?)
- The way the poet creates compound words. (What kind of words? How many? What's the effect?)
- The use of questions. (How much? What kinds of questions? Where in the poem? What's the effect?)
- Plays on words, such as puns and double meanings. (Choose a few examples and explore how they work).

Sharing ideas about the poem on the page

■ In class discussion, talk about what you have discovered about the way the poem looks on the page. Feed back on the aspect of poetic language you chose to focus on in your small group.

Ufo Woman

(pronounced oofoe)

First World meets Third World
Third World meets First World

Mother Earth. Heath Row. Terminal 5. Yo!
Do I look hip in my space-hopper-green
slingbacks, iridescent sky-blue-pink skin
pants and hologram hair cut? Can I have
my clothes back when you've finished with them,
                              please?
Hello! I just got offa the space ship.

I've learnt the language, read the VDU
and watched the video twice. Mother Earth
do *you* read *me*? Why then stamp my passport
ALIEN at Heath Row? Did I come third
in the World Race? Does my iridescent
sky-blue-pink skin embarrass you, mother?

LONDON. Meandering the streets paved with
hopscotch and butterscotch, kids with crystal
cut ice-cream cones and tin can eyes ask 'Why
don't U F O back to your own planet?'
Streets paved with NF (no fun) grafitti
Nefertiti go home from the old days.

So I take a tram, tube, train, taxi trip
hip-hugged, bell-bottomed and thick-lipped,
                              landing
in a crazy crazy cow pat. SUSSEX.
Possibly it's my day-glo afro, rich
as a child paints a tree in full foliage
that makes them stare with flying saucer eyes.

Perhaps my antennae plaits in Winter
naked twigs cocooned in thread for bigger
better hair makes them dare to ask to touch.
'*Can we touch your hair?*' Or not ask at all;
my two-tone hand with its translucent palm,
lifeline, heartline, headline, children, journeys,

prompting the '*Why's it white on the inside
of your hand? Do you wash? Does it wash off?*'
Or my core names. Trochaic, Dactylic,
Galactic beats from ancient poetry,
names they make me repeat, make them call me
those sticks-and-stones-may-break-my-bones-but
names.

In times of need I ask the oracle.
Withdrawing to my work station I press

HELP. I have just two options. HISTORY:
The screen flashes subliminal visuals
from the old days which I quickly translate:
Slave ship:space ship, racism:spacism.

Resignedly I select HERSTORY:
the screen displays a symmetrical tree
which has identical roots and branches.
I can no longer reason, only feel
not aloneness but oneness. I decide
to physically process this data.

So I take the train plane to the Equator
the Motherland, travel 5 degrees North
to the GO SLOW quick-talking fast-living
finger-licking city known as LAGOS.
Streets paved with gold-threaded gold-extensioned
women and silk-suited men; market-stalls

of red, orange, yellow and indigo.
Perhaps it's not my bold wild skin colour,
well camouflaged in this spectrum of life,
but the way I wear my skin, too uptight,
too did-I-wear-the-right-outfit-today?
too I-just-got-off-the-last-London-flight;

or my shy intergalactic lingo
my monospeak, my verbal vertigo
that makes them stare with flying saucer eyes.
They call me Ufo woman, oyinbo
from the old days which translates as weirdo,
white, outsider, other, and I withdraw

into myself, no psychedelic shield,
no chameleonic façade, just raw.
Then I process Ufo and U F O,
realise the former is a blessing:
the latter a curse. I rename myself
Ufo Woman and touch base at Heath Row.

No. Don't bother to strip, drug, bomb search me
I'm not staying this time. Why press rewind?
Why wait for First World homo sapiens
to cease their retroactive spacism?
Their world may be a place worth fighting for
I suggest in the next millennium.
So, smart casual, I prepare for lift off,
in my fibre optic firefly Levis,
my sci-fi hi-fi playing *Revelations*
and my intergalactic mobile ON.
Call me. I'll be surfing the galaxy
Searching for that perfect destination.

Patience Agbabi

Your own live poem   Pair work

In this unit you have seen how two poets use rhythm, rhyme, visual montages and sound, to put across a strong point of view.

■   Work together to compose and perform your own live poem, using the prompts in the box below.

Subject
– Agree on a subject which interests you, such as identity, school, violence, the environment.

Sound
– List ideas, words and phrases which you like the sound of and which are connected to your chosen topic.

Rhythm
– Together try composing a couple of lines and then see if you can set up a rhythm, by changing the odd word, adding in words or moving words around. To help you, look back at the two poems in this section and beat out the rhythm they use.

Rhyme
– Look back at 'Ufo Woman' and 'Breadline' and notice the way that rhyme is used. It usually follows a pattern, often at the end of lines but sometimes internal rhyme is used, where words within lines rhyme with each other.
– Start by listing words on your topic that rhyme with each other. Remember that with long words, it's often just the end of the word that matters. For instance, 'understand' rhymes with anything ending with 'and'.
– Try ending lines with words that rhyme easily.
– Be careful with rhyme! It's got to make sense, or be witty. Just putting in a rhyming word for the sake of it doesn't work at all and is best avoided!

Form
– When you've written four or five lines, see if a form for your poem is emerging (for example, using regular stanzas, or repeating one or two lines in each verse). At this stage, agree what the form is going to be. You could jot down your decisions to help you stick to the pattern.

Other poetic devices
– Make use of other poetic techniques such as alliteration and metaphor.

Re-drafting
– Try reading your poem aloud, with one of you reading and the other listening hard for words or phrases that sound out of place, or rhythms that don't quite work. Go back and make changes, then repeat the process, changing roles.

Presenting your poem   Class work

■   The final product could either be a performance of your poem, a storyboard of your poem or, if your school has the equipment, you could do a video production of it, as a combined poetry and media unit.

Sonnets

In this unit you will:
- learn about the sonnet as a poetic form
- focus closely on a pre-twentieth century and a modern sonnet
- read and talk about a range of different sonnets
- reflect on your reading experience.

Introducing sonnets

Thinking about shapes and forms   Group work

■   Look at the following shapes of poems. See if you can match each shape to its likely purpose. Talk about how you came to your decisions.

C   E   D

A

B

Purposes
- A poem that's telling a story
- A poem that's working through a single argument or idea
- A riddle
- A shape poem
- A haiku

Sonnets

■   Read the description below. Decide on the shape which you think best matches this description.

Sonnets are poems that usually just focus on one idea.

The earliest sonnets were all about love.

The name sonnet came from the Old French for 'little song'.

Sonnets always have fourteen lines.

They usually rhyme.

They are usually written in iambic pentameters - ten syllables to each line, or five beats to each line - though modern poets have experimented with different line lengths and rhythms.

Two kinds of sonnet – getting the facts   Classwork

There are two main forms of sonnet, both of which have 14 lines and rhyme. However, they follow different rhyme schemes.

The Petrarchan, or Italian sonnet typically follows this pattern:
–   8 lines (an octet) asking a question, posing a problem, stating a difficulty or conveying a mood
–   6 lines (a sestet) answering the problem, resolving the problem or difficulty or concluding the mood
–   a rhyme scheme of a-b-b-a-a -b-b-a in the octet and c-d-e-c-d-e or c-d-c-d-c-d in the sestet.

The Shakespearean, or English sonnet, typically follows this pattern:
–   3 four-line units (quatrains). Each four line unit adds a new point in an argument. A quatrain is often just one sentence.
–   1 two-line rhyming unit (a couplet). The couplet often resolves the problem or argument. Sometimes it reverses it.
–   A rhyme scheme, in the quatrains, of a-b-b-a, c-d-d-c, e-f-f-e or a-b-a-b, c-d-c-d, e-f-e-f.

Modern poets writing sonnets sometimes break these rules, having only half-rhymes or no rhyme at all and writing in different rhythms, so that the only thing that marks them out as sonnets is the fact that they have fourteen lines.

In this unit, you will be looking at a range of sonnets, some of which have all the typical features and some of which are more free with the conventions or rules of the sonnet.

But first, check that you understand the sonnet types by doing the activity on the next page.

■ Look at these words which are the line endings of three different sonnets. Decide what kind of sonnet they are, Petrarchan or Shakespearean:

A	B	C
time	trash	strand
night	mattresses	away
prime	fortresses	hand
white	ash	prey
leaves	smash	assay
herd	buttresses	immortalise
sheaves	mistresses	decay
beard	crash	likewise
make	crawl	devise
go	hob	fame
forsake	wall	eternise
grow	job	name
defence	fall	subdue
hence	rob	renew

■ Recap on everything you've learned about the sonnet. Close your books and see how much you can remember.

Experimenting with the structure of a sonnet

To help you get to grips with the form of the Shakespearean, or English sonnet have a go at the activities suggested here.

Constructing an argument   Individual and pair work

■ In pairs, practise putting together an argument in favour of children having part-time jobs. Use the structure outlined here.

- Proposition or main point
- Example or 2nd point
- Example or 3rd point
- Conclusion.

This example shows you how to use this structure.
- Pupils should wear school uniform.
- It's practical – cheap, hard wearing and suitable for school.
- It avoids competition between pupils about who has the most fashionable clothes.
- Therefore it should be introduced into all schools.

■ Now use the same form, but this time the third point should be a challenge to, or disagreement with, the first point. For instance, the uniform argument might now read:

- Pupils should wear school uniform.
- It's practical – cheap, hard wearing and suitable for school.
- But it's very boring and takes away individuality.
- Who cares if it is practical, if it makes everyone look like clones?

Putting the sonnet together again

The lines from two different sonnets have been muddled up and printed below.

■ Use what you know about the structure and rhyme scheme of the sonnet form to help you sort out the lines.

The first lines of each sonnet are:

1. What lips my lips have kissed, and where, and why,

2. My mistress' eyes are nothing like the sun:

What lips my lips have kissed, and where, and why,

Upon the glass and listen for reply,

My mistress, when she walks, treads on the ground:

For unremembered lads that not again

And in my heart there stirs a quiet pain

Nor knows what birds have vanished one by one,

Yet knows its boughs more silent than before:

I love to hear her speak, yet well I know

Will turn to me at midnight with a cry.

My mistress' eyes are nothing like the sun:

I only know that summer sang in me

I cannot say what loves have come and gone,

A little while, that in me sings no more.

If snow be white, why then her breasts are dun:

And yet, by heaven, I think my love as rare

I have forgotten, and what arms have lain

As any she belied with false compare.

I have seen roses damask'd, red and white.

Is full of ghosts tonight, that tap and sigh

If hairs be wires, black wires grow on her head.

Coral is far more red than her lips' red:

That music hath a far more pleasing sound:

And in some perfumes is there more delight

Than in the breath that from my mistress reeks.

But no such roses see I in her cheeks:

I grant I never saw a goddess go,-

Under my head till morning; but the rain

Thus in the winter stands the lonely tree,

■ Share your reconstructed sonnets with the rest of the class. Was there more than one way of putting the lines together, still following the form and rhyme scheme of the Shakespearean sonnet?

The original sonnets are re-printed on pages 122 and 123.

A close focus on a Shakespearean sonnet

The sonnet that you will be reading is by William Shakespeare. The first line is 'When I do count the clock that tells the time'.

Reading the Sonnet   Pair work

■ Talk about what themes you think the sonnet might be exploring.

■ Read the whole poem aloud.

> 12
> When I do count the clock that tells the time,
> And see the brave day sunk in hideous night,
> When I behold the violet past prime,
> And sable curls all silvered o'er with white,
> When lofty trees I see barren of leaves,
> Which erst from heat did canopy the herd,
> And summer's green all girded up in sheaves
> Borne on the bier with white and bristly beard:
> Then of thy beauty do I question make
> That thou among the wastes of time must go,
> Since sweets and beauties do themselves forsake,
> And die as fast as they see others grow,
> >   And nothing 'gainst Time's scythe can make defence
> >   Save breed to brave him when he takes thee hence.

■ Talk about your first responses and your predictions about the themes.

■ Try matching these simplified summaries of the lines to the poem itself. (Some summaries cover more than one line.)

   A   When I see flowers dying

   B   When I see what effect Autumn has on the trees

   C   Then I think about your beauty and realise that, like everything else, it will fade and die

   D   Nothing can prevent time passing

   E   When I see the end of summer, signalled by the way the mown grass has been tied up in bales of hay

   F   Except having a child, who can keep something of you alive after your death

   G   When I see someone's hair turning grey

   H   When I see how time is passing

■   Now talk again about the theme of the poem and try to write a statement about it, starting: 'We think the poem is about ... because ...'

The structure of the sonnet   Class work
The Shakespearean sonnet always has a structure of three quatrains and a couplet.

■   Look at the first word of each section:
When...
When...
Then...
And...

■   Talk about how well the structure of the three quatrains and couplet matches the meaning of the sonnet 'When I do count the clocks'. How does the poet use the structure to *develop* his ideas?

Writing your own sonnet   Individual work
■   Try writing a sonnet with the same structure, using the same first word for each quatrain but choosing your own for the couplet. Choose your own subject, or use one of the ideas below. Try writing it in iambic pentameters (five stressed syllables to each line), if you can.

– Having too much homework
– School uniform
– Part time jobs
– Being in love with someone who just isn't interested
– Feeling alone, even though there are lots of people around
– Feeling sorry about something you've done that can't be mended
– Pollution and urban decay

A close focus on a modern sonnet

You are going to read a sonnet in stages. Like many poems, this one suggests ideas and feelings that can't be pinned down simply. That's what makes poems special, so don't feel that there are quick right and wrong answers. Enjoy exploring different possibilities!

Before reading   Class work
■   First talk about all your associations for the word 'work', and note down your ideas in the form of a spidergram.

■   Talk about all the ways you can think of that the heart has been used as a metaphor. For instance, in the phrase 'home is where the heart is', what do you think the heart represents?

■ Now read the first eight lines of Don Paterson's sonnet:

> My heart was where a hundred dusty roads
> crossed and then ran on; or it was a station
> full of hopeful travellers, though not one
> had either lodgings or a real appointment.
> Whatever it was – my heart, within a day,
> was scattered on a hundred winds, and sped
> through canyons, deserts, river-plains and valleys
> to dark ports, sea-lanes, unmapped continents.

The mood of the poem   Group work

■ Work in fours. One pair should take one of the statements below and see if they can argue for it, using evidence from the poem. The second pair should take the opposite statement.

These lines create a sense of happiness and freedom.

These lines create a sense of sadness and loneliness.

■ Argue against each other.

Exploring the ending

■ Being a sonnet, the poem has another six lines. From what you know about sonnets, predict what you think may happen in these last six lines.

A quick writing experiment   Individual work

■ Try writing the end of the sonnet, in your own way. See if you can follow the style of the first part of the poem.

■ Read each other's endings out loud.

(After the lesson, you could write out the sonnets, written jointly by you and Don Paterson, to be displayed on the classroom wall.)

The last six lines   Group work

■ Now read Don Paterson's ending. You are going to explore what you think is happening in the last six lines and what mood is created. To do this follow the instructions below.

> But now, like a swarm returning to the hive
> at that purple hour when all the crows go hoarse
> and sail off to the crags and the black eaves,
> my heart turns to its melancholy work
> with honey gathered from a hundred flowers
> and the hundred sorrows of the gathering dark.

- First, see if you can find the main clause in the sentence, by looking for a finite verb and its subject. Talk about how this main clause marks a change from the first part of the poem.

- The rest of the six lines is an extended simile for what the 'heart' is like. Talk about what the simile is, and follow it through the poem, tracing how it works.

- Each group should now take responsibility for looking closely at *one* of these phrases, analysing very closely the effect of particular words, what mood they create and why:

a hundred dusty roads

like a swarm returning to the hive

at that purple hour

when all the crows go hoarse

and sail off to the crags and the black eaves

my heart turns to its melancholy work

with honey gathered from a hundred flowers

and the hundred sorrows of the gathering dark

Sharing and developing your ideas   Class work
- As a whole class, listen to each group's views and pool your ideas on the effect of the ending.

The title
- Now read the complete poem, printed on the next page and note down your personal response.

Exploring form and structure

The Work

My heart was where a hundred dusty roads
crossed and then ran on; or it was a station
full of hopeful travellers, though not one
had either lodgings or a real appointment.
Whatever it was – my heart, within a day,
was scattered on a hundred winds, and sped
through canyons, deserts, river-plains and valleys
to dark ports, sea-lanes, unmapped continents.

But now, like a swarm returning to the hive
at that purple hour when all the crows go hoarse
and sail off to the crags and the black eaves,
my heart turns to its melancholy work
with honey gathered from a hundred flowers
and the hundred sorrows of the gathering dark.

Don Paterson

A conventional sonnet?

- Remind yourself of the 'rules' of a typical Petrarchan and Shakespearean sonnet. Look at the structure of 'The Work,' and what it does with rhyme and rhythm.

- Talk about the ways in which Don Paterson has used and adapted the sonnet form. How effective do you think it is, as a sonnet?

Writing about the poem   Individual work

- Read this KS3 pupil's comment on the poem. Do you agree or disagree? Did you read it differently?

I like the way the poet uses unusual images, not what you'd normally expect. The images of the dusty roads make you think of America's barren deserts. I think you can feel the sadness, even though it doesn't actually say, 'I was feeling sad.' I like the sense of mystery in it. Some of the first part of the poem, such as speeding 'through the canyons, deserts, river-plains and valleys' indicates the excitement of travelling through unknown places, 'unmapped continents' but the idea of his heart being like a station full of travellers with no home or connections suggests the loneliness of being away from home.
The ending is full of mixed feelings - the image of bees returning to the hive suggests homecoming and the 'honey gathered from a hundred flowers' sounds

hopeful but the ending of the poem, 'the hundred sorrows of the gathering dark' leaves you with a feeling of loss and sadness.
I'm not sure why it's called 'The Work'. Could the work be the poetry he writes? Does he need to have experiences of travel and sadness to be able to write sad poems? Is this why he describes his work as 'melancholy'? Or maybe it's just that his heart isn't happy anywhere, either travelling the world or settling down to ordinary life?

- ■ Write a short essay drawing on everything you have discussed about 'The Work'. Write about some of these issues:
  - what you thought it was about
  - the mood and how it was created
  - the way it developed from the first eight lines to the last six lines
  - the way the images (metaphors and similes) worked
  - any lines or phrases that you particularly liked and what made them special for you
  - how it worked as a sonnet.

Don't forget to take out short quotations, to analyse in depth, as a way of digging deeper into the poem and exploring how it works.

A sonnet for the radio

On pages 122-125 you will find seven more sonnets. You will be working on the following scenario:

> As part of its new education brief Virgin FM is producing a short programme about poetry, focusing on different poetic forms. You are a member of the team working on the programme. You have been asked to select just one poem to represent the sonnet form. You will have to argue for your choice in the team meeting.

Reading the sonnets   Group work
But first, to prepare for this, you will be reading all of the sonnets in small groups, talking about them and making some quick comparisons.

- ■ Divide the sonnets up between you. Each of you will end up reading one or two. On your own, prepare a reading of your sonnets. Check words you can't pronounce, with each other or your teacher, then practise reading them aloud. Try to:
  - make it fluent
  - vary your tone of voice
  - pause for emphasis, or where there is a punctuation mark
  - read quite slowly, enjoying the sound of the words.

- ■ Take turns to read your sonnets aloud to each other.

Comparing the sonnets

■ Begin to think about similarities and differences between the sonnets, in a very general way. At this stage, don't worry too much about understanding all the detail. Use a chart like the one below to help you. Put ticks in the columns, if they apply. One or two have been entered for you, as examples.

	My mistress' eyes	Glasgow sonnet	'What lips my lips have kissed'	'One day I wrote her name'	Needle Work	North (west) ern	'When I have fears'
Modern		√					
Pre-20thC.	√						
Petrarchan							
Shakespearean	√						
Adapts the traditional forms							
An argument							
An idea							
A mood or description							
Uses the sonnet form humorously							

Sharing ideas   Class work

■ Talk about what you've discovered about the similarities and differences between the sonnets.

■ Go on to talk about whether there are differences between the twentieth century and pre-twentieth century sonnets, both in the way they use the sonnet form and in the subjects they write about. Why might there be these differences?

Background research Pair work

You could look in more detail at the relationship between the sonnet and the time and place in which it was written. To do this you will need to do some background research.

■ In pairs, take responsibility for finding out about the poet, the place and historical period in which they lived and wrote.

■ Talk together about any connections you have noticed between the sonnet (the text) and the context.

■   Take it in turns to give a short report summarising your discoveries.

Choosing a sonnet for the radio programme

■   You should now be ready to spend some time choosing a sonnet. Think about some of these issues:

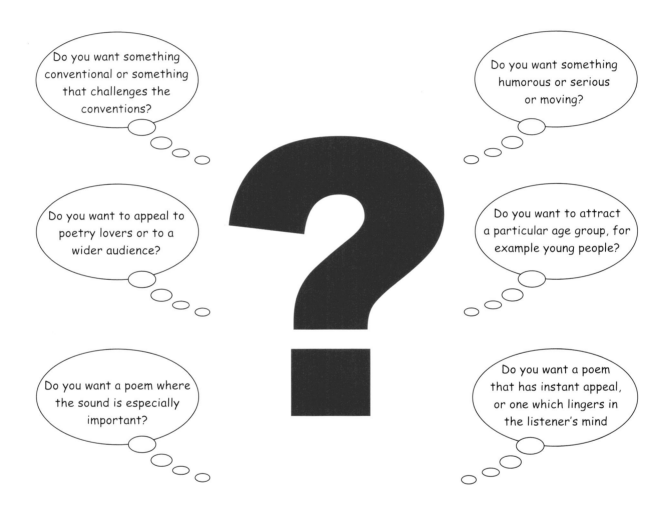

Do you want something conventional or something that challenges the conventions?

Do you want something humorous or serious or moving?

Do you want to appeal to poetry lovers or to a wider audience?

Do you want to attract a particular age group, for example young people?

Do you want a poem where the sound is especially important?

Do you want a poem that has instant appeal, or one which lingers in the listener's mind

■   Once you have chosen a sonnet, use the framework below to explore it in more detail.

- What kind of sonnet is it? (Use the chart to remind you.)
- What is it about?
- How does it use the sonnet structure to develop an idea or argument or mood?
- What do you like about the language – the sounds of words, the way the poet plays with words, the use of rhyme, the rhythm and so on?
- In what ways has the poet used images to convey an idea or argument or mood?
- What made you choose it – what's interesting, or enjoyable or special about it?
- If it's a pre-twentieth century poem, in what ways do you think it still speaks to

Exploring form and structure

us today? Why do you think it's worth presenting a poem written so long ago?
- Why would it be a particularly good choice for the radio programme?

The team meeting   Group work

■   Join up with two or three other pairs, who have chosen different poems. (You should now be in groups of 6-8). You will be the team planning the programme. Present your poems to each other, arguing for your choices. Listen to the other groups with an open mind, hearing their views, arguments and explanations of their poems.

The final decision

■   At the end of the presentations, see if you can reach agreement about which poem should be chosen for the programme. Make a list of points in favour of the poems which people think are most suitable for the radio programme.

■   Prepare a brief report about your discussion.

■   Compare decisions across the class, to see if there is one poem that stands out as being more popular than the others.

Writing about the sonnets   Individual work

■   Choose one of these ways of writing about the sonnets that you have read:

- Write about one sonnet that you now feel you know very well. Comment on your personal response to it, the way it develops and what it does with the form that is especially interesting.

- Write a personal account of all the reading that you have done for this unit. It can be chatty and informal but it shouldn't be too general – try to make some comments about what you liked or disliked about particular poems, or what you learned, using detailed examples to explain what you mean.

These sentence starters might help you to begin to structure your writing:

When I realised that we were going to read sonnets, I thought ... I expected sonnets to be ...

Reading the first Shakespeare sonnet, this view was/was not confirmed. It was ...

Of all the sonnets we read, my favourite is ... Whereas many of the sonnets are ..., this one is ...

As a poetic form, the sonnet is particularly good for expressing ...

My mistress' eyes are nothing like the sun

My mistress' eyes are nothing like the sun;
Coral is far more red than her lips' red;
If snow be white, why then her breasts are dun;
If hairs be wires, black wires grow on her head.
I have seen roses damasked, red and white,
But no such roses see I in her cheeks,
And in some perfumes is there more delight
Than in the breath that from my mistress reeks.
I love to hear her speak, yet well I know
That music hath a far more pleasing sound;
I grant I never saw a goddess go –
My mistress when she walks treads on the ground.
    And yet, by heaven, I think my love as rare
    As any she belied with false compare.

Shakespeare

Glasgow Sonnet

A mean wind wanders through the backcourt trash.
Hackles on puddles rise, old mattresses
puff briefly and subside. Play-fortresses
of brick and bric-a-brac spill out some ash.
Four storeys have no windows left to smash,
but in the fifth a chipped sill buttresses
mother and daughter the last mistresses
of that black block condemned to stand, not crash.
Around them the cracks deepen, the rats crawl.
The kettle whimpers on a crazy hob.
Roses of mould grow from ceiling to wall.
The man lies late since he has lost his job,
smokes on one elbow, letting his coughs fall
thinly into an air too poor to rob.

Edwin Morgan

Exploring form and structure

Sonnet XIii

What lips my lips have kissed, and where, and why,
I have forgotten, and what arms have lain
Under my head till morning; but the rain
Is full of ghosts tonight, that tap and sigh
Upon the glass and listen for reply,
And in my heart there stirs a quiet pain
For unremembered lads that not again
Will turn to me at midnight with a cry.
Thus in the winter stands the lonely tree,
Nor knows what birds have vanished one by one,
Yet knows its boughs more silent than before:
I cannot say what loves have come and gone,
I only know that summer sang in me
A little while, that in me sings no more.

Edna St. Vincent Millay

'One day I wrote her name upon the strand'

One day I wrote her name upon the strand,
  But came the waves and washed it away:
Again I wrote it with a second hand,
  But came the tide and made my pains his prey.
  Vain man (said she), that dost in vain assay
A mortal thing so to immortalise;
  For I myself shall like to this decay,
And eke my name be wiped out likewise.
Not so (quod I); let baser things devise
  To die in dust, but you shall live by fame;
My verse your virtues rare shall eternise,
  And in the heavens write your glorious name:
      Where, whenas death shall all the world subdue,
      Our love shall live, and later life renew.

Edmund Spenser

Needle Work

I am the genius at the heart of things,
The answer at the middle of the maze,
Secret cartographer who tugs the strings,
The arrow that goes nowhere, but obeys
Earth's headstrong pull. North, south, east, west,
And all their subdivisions heed my mark;
The pioneers, the other-world-obsessed,
Follow from Erebus to Noah's Ark
My scarlet finger in the glassy box,
Directing humans through geography,
Through Roaring Forties to the fish-paved docks,
Through unmapped deserts to the tourists' sea.

But touch me not. Unless I'm free to roam,
You'll never set the course that brings you home.

U.A. Fanthorpe

North(west)ern

I was twelve as in the 12-bar blues, sick
for the Southeast, marooned on the North Wales coast,
a crotchet, my tongue craving the music
of Welsh, Scouse or Manc; entering the outpost
of Colwyn Bay Pier, midsummer, noon,
niteclub for those of us with the deep ache
of adolescence, when I heard that tune.
Named it in one. Soul. My heart was break

dancing on the road to Wigan Casino,
Northern Soul mecca, where transatlantic bass
beat blacker than blue in glittering mono

then back via Southport, Rhyl to the time, place
I bit the Big Apple. Black. Impatient. Young.
A string of pips exploding on my tongue.

Patience Agbabi

Exploring form and structure

'When I have fears that I may cease to be'

When I have fears that I may cease to be
  Before my pen has glean'd my teeming brain,
Before high-piled books, in charactery,
  Hold like rich garners the full ripen'd grain;
When I behold, upon the nights starr'd face,
  Huge cloudy symbols of a high romance,
And think that I may never live to trace
  Their shadows, with the magic hand of chance;
And when I feel, fair creature of an hour,
  That I shall never look upon thee more,
Never have relish in the faery power
  Of unreflecting love; – then on the shore
Of the wide world I stand alone, and think
Till love and fame to nothingness do sink.

John Keats

Sophie Hannah

A poem from a painting

The poet Sophie Hannah was given a postcard of a painting by Georgio de Chirico as a stimulus for writing a poem. This painting is reproduced below.

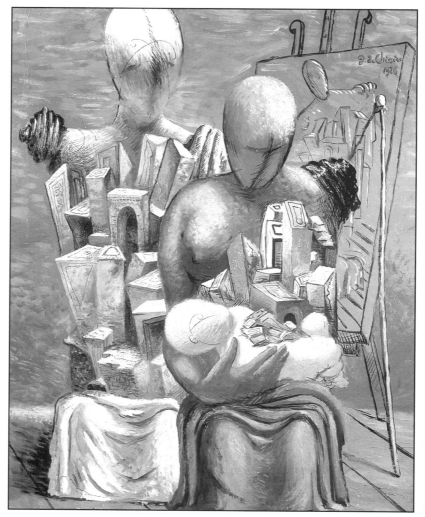

The Painter's Family (La Famille du Peintre), 1926 (Oil on canvas, support 1464mm x 1149mm) by Georgio de Chirico (1888-1978), © DACS 2001

Thinking about the painting   Individual and class work

■   Look closely at the painting and talk about what you see. Talk about any ideas suggested to you by the painting. Use the prompts given here to start you thinking.

  - Tell each other stories or anecdotes from your own experience that the painting reminds you of.
  - Share ideas and words to do with the mood created by the painting.
  - Share words or phrases to describe what you see in the painting (shapes, colours and so on).
  - Tell the story of the painting.
  - Create thought bubbles and speech bubbles for each of the figures in the painting.

■   Choose one of these ideas or angles and spend five minutes drafting the first few lines of a poem.

■   Share some of the first lines as a whole class. Talk about how you went about writing your lines. What were you thinking about most while you were writing?

| the ideas | the sounds | using rhyme | being descriptive |

| using metaphors or similes | sounding poetic | being funny | telling a story |

| getting something down on paper fast | how difficult it felt |

| getting across a mood or emotion | something else |

Sophie Hannah's ideas      Class viewing and pair work

■   Listen to the poet, Sophie Hannah, talking about the painting and her idea for a poem about it. Listen to her reading the first full draft of this poem.

■   Read the poem printed on the next page. Talk about your first impressions and ideas. What do you find interesting or surprising or enjoyable or striking about what she came up with? You could think about the subject, point of view, use of rhythm, rhyme, repetition and so on.

An unpublished first draft of a rondel

At first he could be anybody's child
Sadly, for him, he happens to be yours.
Within a week or two, you'll get your claws
Into his character. Today, he smiled

As if he couldn't see that you're compiled
Of defects, grudges, grievances and flaws.
At first he could be anybody's child
Sadly, for him, he happens to be yours.

Perhaps I'll kidnap him, let him run wild,
Try leaving him at friendly strangers' doors,
Women who've lost their only sons in wars,

Before you have him washed and cut and styled
At first he could be anybody's child
Sadly, for him, he happens to be yours.

Watching the drafting process Class viewing and pair work

Sophie Hannah was filmed in the process of drafting the poem.

■ Watch the video clip showing her thinking through the beginning of the poem and one line in the second stanza.

■ Now look at the draft printed below.

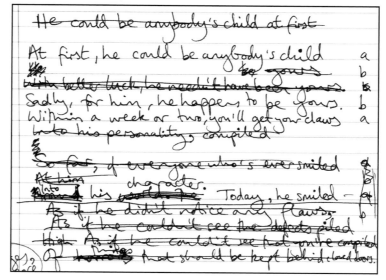

The writing process

■ Talk about what you found interesting about the way she went about writing the poem and the changes she made.

You might think about:
- how long it took her to write the first stanza
- how much she changed as she went along
- what made her choose one word rather than another and how she knew whether it felt 'right' or not
- what she paid most attention to.

■ From what she says, what is she thinking about most as she drafts the poem? How does this compare with your thoughts when writing?

■ Feed back your thoughts to the class.

The form of the poem Classwork and class viewing

In the video interview, Sophie Hannah talks about writing in a formal verse form. The definitions of some of the poetic terms she uses are given here.

■ Before you watch the video, read through the definitions. Make sure you understand what each one means by talking about them as a class.

End-stopped line: a line which ends with a definite break or pause, compared with a run-on line with no pause at the end of the line. This is shown by a punctuation mark, like a comma, full stop, colon or semi-colon.

Scan/scansion: the rhythm of a line is based on the number of beats in it. This depends on how many syllables there are and which ones are stressed (accented). For instance, in the line,

/ / / / /
They flee from me that sometime did me seek,

the five stressed syllables are marked with a slash. If you alter the pattern of stresses, it can mess up the rhythm of the poem. For instance, if you wrote:

They flee from me that once did me seek

it interrupts the pattern and makes it sound awkward. It's important to read a poem aloud while you're writing it, to check what it sounds like.
A poem is said to 'scan' well, if you keep to the rhythmic pattern.

Refrain: a phrase or line that is repeated in a poem is called a refrain
(rather like a chorus in a song).

The writing process

■ Listen to Sophie Hannah talking about why she likes using formal verse forms, with strict rhyme schemes and rhythm, rather than free verse. Make a note of anything which interests you and share these points with the rest of the class.

More poems by Sophie Hannah

This chapter includes ideas for work on the poems Sophie Hannah reads and talks about on the video. Some of the work focuses on reading, talking and writing about the poems, while other poems in the unit are explored as models for your own writing.

'Nothing Gold Can Stay'

The shape of a poem   Class work

■ You are going to read a poem called 'Nothing Gold Can Stay'. The shape of the poem is shown in the outline below. The last words of each line are as follows: gold; hold; flower; hour; leaf; grief; day and stay.

■ Talk about your expectations of the poem. You could think abut the structure of the poem, its subject, its mood and its themes.

Reading 'Nothing Gold Can Stay'   Pair work

■ Read the whole poem aloud. Use the prompts on the next page to help you talk about it.

> ## Nothing Gold Can Stay
>
> Nature's first green is gold,
> Her hardest hue to hold.
> Her early leaf's a flower;
> But only so an hour.
> Then leaf subsides to leaf.
> So Eden sank to grief,
> So dawn goes down to day.
> Nothing gold can stay.
>
> **Robert Frost**

- What are your first thoughts and feelings about the poem?
- What can you say for sure about it?
- Look at each line closely and talk about a range of possible interpretations.
- Now talk about what you think the poem is about.
- Talk about how it works for you. For instance, do you like the ideas, the length of the poem, the use of rhyme, the sound of the words, the rhythm or the vocabulary? Try to be very precise in explaining exactly what you liked and why, using examples from the poem to show what you mean.

■   Take it in turns to feed back your ideas. Make a note of anything which you had not already thought of.

Sophie Hannah reads 'Nothing Gold Can Stay   Class viewing

'Nothing Gold Can Stay' is one of Sophie Hannah's favourite poems. She wrote a poem of her own inspired by it.

■   Listen to her reading Robert Frost's poem and talking about it on the video.

■   Then listen to her poem and her comments about the writing of it.

Sophie Hannah's poem   Pair and class work

■   Look at Sophie Hannah's poem in more detail and talk about your first responses.

Trainers All Turn Grey

(*after Robert Frost's* 'Nothing Gold Can Stay')

You buy your trainers new.
They cost a bob or two.
At first they're clean and white,
The laces thick and tight.
Then they must touch the ground –
(You have to walk around).
You learn to your dismay
Trainers all turn grey.

■   Use the chart on the next page to look at the ways in which she follows the style and ideas in the first poem and the ways in which she adapts them to create something very different. The chart has been started for you, to give you some idea of the kinds of things you could say.

	Nothing Gold Can Stay	Trainers All Turn Grey
Subject	Nature, the seasons	
Themes	Time passing, how everything fades or dies	
Rhyme Scheme Line Length and rhythm	3 beats to a bar (3 stressed syllables)	
Tone		
Vocabulary	Lots of words with one syllable which makes it seem simple	
The title		
Anything else		

■ Take it in turns to report back what you have discovered about the poems.

Writing a poem of your own Homework

■ Try writing your own poem based on the two you have read, in which you follow the same pattern but with a twist of your own.

Your poem must have:
  - 8 lines
  - an aa, bb, cc, dd rhyme scheme
  - 3 beats per line
  - a simple subject which explores a theme (like loss, death, the way that nothing lasts forever, the difference between the generations and so on).

It could:
  - be serious or witty
  - use modern and colloquial (everyday) language or poetic language
  - be based on something in your life or on a more abstract idea.

Exploring 'Your Dad Did What?'

Reading the poem   Class viewing

■ Watch the video clip where Sophie Hannah introduces and reads this poem.

■ Sort out what's happening in the poem by annotating it with:
  - the voice of the narrator
  - the voice of the teacher
  - what the boy writes.

■ Talk about the poem and your response. You should consider the following points:
  - the teacher's attitude towards the boy
  - the use of rhyme in the poem
  - the final verse of the poem.

Your Dad Did What?

Where they have been, if they have been away,
or what they've done at home, if they have not –
you make them write about the holiday.
One writes *My Dad did*. What? Your Dad did what?

That's not a sentence. Never mind the bell.
We stay behind until the work is done.
You count their words (you who can count and spell);
all the assignments are complete bar one

and though this boy seems bright, that one is his.
He says he's finished, doesn't want to add
anything, hands it in just as it is.
No change. *My Dad did*. What? What did his Dad?

You find the 'E' you gave him as you sort
through reams of what this girl did, what that lad did,
and read the line again, just one 'e' short:
This holiday was horrible. My Dad did.

The role of the reader   Group work

■ Use the questions below to focus your discussion about the poem and what Sophie Hannah is doing in it.

  - What point do you think Sophie Hannah is making in the poem?
  - At what stage in the poem did you understand the point being made?
  - Sophie Hannah does not make the point of the poem obvious. What does she expect the reader to be able to do?
  - How effective do you find poetry, and rhyming poetry in particular, to make a serious point?

A reader's responses

Printed below is a short extract from one reader's response.

■ Read it and use it to help you make a few statements about your own responses.

> I found this poem very moving. This was partly because of the way Sophie Hannah leaves the reader to work out what has happened to the boy's dad. I didn't understand it at first and had to read it several times.

Collecting ideas   Class work

■ Collect together the responses from the different groups. Your teacher will write these on the board or OHT.

■ Try integrating quotations from the poem into your responses. Add explorations of these quotations, analysing the techniques Sophie Hannah uses. For instance:

statement: Sophie Hannah creates a clear picture of a teacher.

statement with quotation incorporated: Sophie Hannah creates a clear picture of a teacher who is confident and busy, with the line, 'That's not a sentence. Never mind the bell.'

statement with quotation incorporated plus analysis: Sophie Hannah creates a clear picture of a teacher who is confident and busy, with the phrase, 'That's not a sentence. Never mind the bell.' She uses short sentences to suggest snappiness and impatience.

Planning a written response

■ Talk about ways you could organise your responses into a written essay, including ways of beginning and ending it and phrases to start new paragraphs.

Writing a first draft   Homework

■ Write a first draft of a short essay analysing the poem and giving your personal response to it.

Exploring 'Ticket to Staines'

Listening to the poem   Class viewing

■ Watch Sophie Hannah introducing and reading 'Ticket to Staines'.

■ Make a note of your first response to the poem and to Sophie Hannah's comments on it.

A debate   Group work

■ Printed below are two views of the poem.

> A comic poem – just a piece of light entertainment

> A poem with a serious message

■ Work in small groups, with half the groups taking one view and the other half taking the other. Find evidence from the poem to back up the view you are arguing for. You might want to look at some of these issues in making your case:
  - tone
  - vocabulary
  - the way the poem starts and ends
  - the title
  - the use of rhythm and rhyme.

Ticket to Staines

I'd emerged from the second of two freezing trains
With a bag full of cheese salad sandwich remains
When I met a tree surgeon who said he was broke
And asked me to buy him a ticket to Staines.

He told me a jumbled, unfortunate tale
About how he had broken the terms of his bail
And he had to get back to his Mum's before ten
Or the cops would be taking him straight back to jail.

He told me his story outside Euston station
Describing his crime and its justification:
His tree surgeon's chainsaw had sliced through a train
In an effort to sabotage veal transportation.

His Mum had lumbago and no credit card
For a telephone booking. I thought long and hard
And it seemed to be me and me only that stood
Between him and a grilling at New Scotland Yard.

With diminishing faith in the state of my brains
And without quite condoning the slicing of trains
I led him past Knickerbox, Sock Shop and all
And bought that tree surgeon a ticket to Staines.

What will become of him? Where will he go?
(And don't say, 'You paid for it, you ought to know.')
I mean, is there a place for him? Is there a place
For a lawbreaking tree surgeon, chainsaw in tow?

There's a place for the tyrant who rules and constrains,
For the person who keeps other people in chains.
Wherever that tree surgeon goes, freedom reigns.
I wish I could see him arriving in Staines.

Staging the debate   Class work
- Hear the arguments from both sides of the debate and make a record of the points the speakers make in support of the position they have taken.

A poetry writing suggestion   Homework
- Try writing the tree surgeon's version of the story, in which he meets a young woman who tells him that she's a poet. He asks her for the money for a ticket to Staines. Decide whether you think his story is true and include his views about the young woman, his own situation and what happens to him after this meeting. If you can, use the same rhyme scheme as the original (aaba). When you've written the first line of each stanza, make a list of all the words that you might be able to use in the other rhyming lines.

Standing by Burger King, her head in a book,
She wasn't the sort to have time for a crook.

Rhymes with look, cook, crook, rook, brook

Writing a poem 1 – 'Symptoms'

'Symptoms' is an example of a list poem. This is a simple but effective way of expressing your ideas in the form of a poem.

Watching the video   Class viewing
- Watch the video of Sophie Hannah talking about this poem and reading it aloud. As you listen make a note of the main points she makes about the poem and the way she wrote it.

'Symptoms'   Pair work
- Look at the poem on the next page and talk about the structure and how effective it is. Try coming up with a short summary of the patterning in the poem to share as a class.

The writing process

Symptoms

Although you have given me a stomach upset,
weak knees, a lurching heart, a fuzzy brain,
a high-pitched laugh, a monumental phone bill,
a feeling of unworthiness, sharp pain
when you are somewhere else, a guilty conscience,
a longing, and a dread of what's in store,
a pulse rate for the *Guinness Book of Records* –
life now is better than it was before.

Although you have given me a raging temper,
insomnia, a rising sense of panic,
a hopeless challenge, bouts of introspection,
raw, bitten nails, a voice that's strangely manic,
a selfish streak, a fear of isolation,
a silly smile, lips that are chapped and sore,
a running joke, a risk, an inspiration –
life now is better than it was before.

Although you have given me a premonition,
chattering teeth, a goal, a lot to lose,
a granted wish, mixed motives, superstitions,
hang-ups and headaches, fear of awful news,
a bubble in my throat, a dare to swallow,
a crack of light under a closing door,
the crude, fantastic prospect of forever –
life now is better than it was before.

■   Talk about what view of love the poem gives. Decide whether you agree or disagree
with these statements. Explore your reasons in detail.

- The poem is anti-sentimental.
- Being in love is ghastly.
- Despite all the suffering that love brings, it's all worth it in the end.
- The poem plays on the idea of being 'love-sick'.
- The list pattern makes the poem humorous.
- The list pattern shows just how much love can make you suffer.
- The contrast between the list and the refrain at the end of each stanza shows
  the two sides of being in love.

Feedback   Class work
■   Collect together your ideas about the poem in whole class discussion.

Writing a list poem   Individual work

■   Think of your own idea for a list poem with a refrain. You could use the same pattern, starting 'Although'. Use the ideas suggested here to start you thinking.

- A poem about parents
- A poem about a brother or sister
- A poem about money
- A poem about computer games, or *EastEnders* or sport on TV
- A poem about food, eating or dieting
- A poem about adolescence

■   Decide on the point you want to make and write a first draft of the refrain (the last line of each verse).

■   Brainstorm words and phrases which suggest that the opposite of this point is true.

■   Experiment by arranging these words and phrases in different ways. Use a variety of techniques, for example, alliteration, rhyme, rhythm and so on.

Getting feedback   Pair work

■   Help each other draft your poems, suggesting other words and phrases and different ways of arranging them.

■   Finish writing the final version of your poem, in the light of the feedback you received.

Reading your poems   Group or class work

■   Take it in turns to read your poems out loud.

Writing a poem 2 – 'Early Bird Blues'

Listening to the poem   Class viewing

'Early Bird Blues' takes a well known proverb and plays around with it, turning it on its head.

■   Talk about the proverb, 'The early bird catches the worm'. What does it mean to you?

■   Watch Sophie Hannah on video performing the poem and listen to her talking about it.

Early Bird Blues

I am the early bird.
I have worn out my shoes
Simply because I heard
First come was first to choose.
One of my talents is avoiding queues.

I never ask how long
I shall be made to wait.
I have done nothing wrong.
I don't exaggerate.
To state the obvious, I'm never late.

Why has the queue not grown?
Nobody hears me speak.
I stand here all alone
Which makes me look unique
But even so, the worm avoids my beak.

What do the others know?
Have I been told a lie?
Why don't I turn and go?
I still know how to fly,
But, damn, I want that worm. I don't know why.

- Talk about what the poem does with the proverb. You may want to discuss:
  - who the speaker in the poem is
  - whether the poem backs up or contradicts the proverb
  - what the effect is (Comic? Sad? Serious? A mixture?)

Talking about proverbs　Class work
A selection of common proverbs are printed below.

- Read the proverbs and suggest any others you know, perhaps from different cultures.

Too many cooks spoil the broth	It's no use crying over spilt milk
Every cloud has a silver lining	Absence makes the heart grow fonder
A stitch in time saves nine	Waste not want not
Don't count your chickens before they hatch	You can't have your cake and eat it
Out of sight, out of mind	People in glass houses shouldn't throw stones
Many hands make light work	The darkest hour is just before the dawn
A bird in the hand is worth two in the bush	The pot calling the kettle black

- Talk about what the proverbs really mean and suggest ways you could play with these meanings.

Writing a poem Individual and group work

- Choose one of the proverbs to use as a starting-point for a poem. You could use Sophie Hannah's strategy of talking in the voice of one of the characters in the proverb, or turning the message of the proverb on its head.

- Read your poems out loud and help each other with any sections which don't work or are proving a problem.

Writing for revenge

Listening to the poems – 'Differences' and 'If People Disapprove of You'

Class viewing

- Watch Sophie Hannah talking about what prompted her to write these two poems and listen to her reading the poems aloud.

Differences

Not everyone who wears a hat
Is copying the Queen.
Not everything that's large and flat
Thinks it's a movie screen.
If every time I dress in blue
I imitate the sea,
It makes no difference what I do –
Nothing is down to me.

Not every dim, electric light
Would like to be the sun.
A water pistol doesn't quite
Mimic a loaded gun.
I do my best, I do my worst
With my specific heart –
God and the Devil got there first;
They had an early start.

Tomatoes can be round and red
Yet be distinct from Mars.
Not all the things above my head
Can be described as stars.
The world had better learn what's what
(If it remotely cares) –
A ladder is a ladder, not
A failed attempt at stairs.

The writing process

If People Disapprove of You...

Make being disapproved of your hobby.
Make being disapproved of your aim.
Devise new ways of scoring points
In the Being Disapproved Of Game.

Let them disapprove in their dozens.
Let them disapprove in their hoards.
You'll find that being disapproved of
Builds character, brings rewards.

Just like any form of striving.
Don't be arrogant; don't coast
On your high disapproval rating.
Try to be disapproved of most.

At this point, if it's useful,
Draw a pie chart or a graph.
Show it to someone who disapproves.
When they disapprove, just laugh.

Count the emotions you provoke:
Anger, suspicion, shock.
One point for each of these and two
For every boat you rock.

Feel yourself warming to your task –
You do it bloody well.
At last you've found an area
In which you can excel.

Savour the thrill of risk without
The fear of getting caught.
Whether they sulk or scream or pout,
Enjoy your new-found sport.

Meanwhile, all those who disapprove
While you are having fun
Won't even know your game exists
So tell yourself you've won.

Both of these poems are 'revenge' poems. Sophie Hannah wrote them in the spirit of:
- complaint
- annoyance
- getting her own back
- humorous ridiculing of the people who've annoyed her
- standing up for herself
- defiance.

Exploring a poem in detail   Pair work

■   Take responsibility for looking more closely at one of these poems.

■   Explore what aspects of the language and style create this defiant tone. You might want to think about some of the issues below.

- Negatives (How much are words like 'not' or 'no' used? What is the effect of this?)
- Sentences (Are there lots of questions, statements, commands or exclamations? What is the effect of this?)
- Vocabulary (What kinds of words does she use? Do any words leap out at you as being particularly strong or different or interesting?)
- Exaggeration (Does the poet make her point more forcefully by exaggerating things? If so, how?)
- Images (What kinds of metaphors or similes does she use? To what effect?)

Comparing poems   Group and class work

■   Join up with a pair who looked at the other poem. Introduce your poem to each other.

■   Compare the different ways Sophie Hannah creates the negative tone in the two poems. Draw together anything they have in common and agree three points to feed back in class discussion.

Writing your own poem   Homework

■   Write your own 'revenge' poem, in which you have the final word, take a defiant stand or stick up for yourself, for example, 'Why should I put up with being bossed around by my family?'

Sophie Hannah– the poet speaks

A poetry reading  Class viewing
- Listen to Sophie Hannah reading the poems you have not yet heard. Make a note of anything you notice about them and how they compare with the ones you've been working on.

- Watch Sophie Hannah on video, talking about what sort of poet she is. As you listen make a note of any points which you think are interesting or important.

- Take it in turns to read out points from your notes. Your teacher will collect together the main points you make and write them on the board or OHT. Pull together all your ideas about what makes Sophie Hannah's poetry special.

Writing an introduction   Individual work
- Produce an introduction to Sophie Hannah's work for one of these different audiences:
  - a short feature on a new radio review programme for teenagers, on books, films, TV and music
  - a short article about Sophie Hannah's work for a new magazine on English, designed for KS3 pupils, to be distributed free to all schools
  - a talk in a school assembly, preparing your Year Group for a visit to the school by Sophie Hannah later in the term.

Your introduction should include:
  - a few short extracts from her poems
  - comments on what makes her poems interesting or unusual or entertaining
  - anything you know or can find out about who she is and how she became a poet
  - any other ideas you have for bringing her poems to life and making your feature lively and interesting.